Guidance for the Verification and Validation of Neural Networks

Guidance for the Verification and Validation of Neural Networks

Laura L. Pullum
Brian J. Taylor
Majorie A. Darrah

IEEE
COMPUTER
SOCIETY

BICENTENNIAL
1807
WILEY
2007
BICENTENNIAL

A Wiley-Interscience Publication
JOHN WILEY & SONS, INC.

Published by John Wiley & Sons, Inc., Hoboken, New Jersey.
Published simultaneously in Canada.

For general information on our other products and services or for technical support, please contact our Customer Care Department within the United States at (800) 762-2974, outside the United States at (317) 572-3993 or fax (317) 572-4002.

Wiley also publishes its books in a variety of electronic formats. Some content that appears in print may not be available in electronic format. For information about Wiley products, visit our web site at www.wiley.com.

Library of Congress Cataloging-in-Publication Data is available.

ISBN-13: 978-0-470-08457-1
ISBN-10: 0-470-08457-X

Printed in the United States of America.

10 9 8 7 6 5 4 3 2 1

CONTENTS

PREFACE

At NASA, adaptive systems have left the experimental stage and are now becoming a practical solution to the demands of our technological goals for many of our projects, including those with high criticality and dependability. Neural networks are a logical development and operational solution to adaptive system applications and, as such, NASA needs to understand these systems and assure them. This guidebook provides the necessary direction and insight to do both.

The research and work by researchers at the Institute for Scientific Research, Inc. (ISR) that has gone into this guide was sponsored by the NASA Office of Safety and Mission Assurance through its Independent Verification and Validation (IV&V) Facility. A companion to the book *Methods and Procedures for the Verification and Validation of Artificial Neural Networks* [Taylor 2005], this guidance book takes the methods and procedures work and brings it to the practitioner level. This work is not only for V&V but for all software assurance and software engineering practitioners. It provides a basic overview of neural networks before expanding and adapting the application of normal software validation and verification processes to those systems that contain neural networks. Starting with verification and validation basics in the *IEEE Standard for Software Verification and Validation, IEEE Std 1012-1998* [IEEE 1998], this guidebook augments those requirements, providing extrapolations where needed and solid examples.

Whereas *Methods and Procedures for the Verification and Validation of Artificial Neural Networks* contains a series of monographs discussing and advancing the process of verification and validation of neural networks, the authors aimed this guidebook toward the practitioner, with down-to-earth "how to's" as well as cautions for dealing with the various aspects of these adaptive systems. Chapter 2 discuses the features of various types of neural networks and their applicability to a design solution, and then provides assurance tools and techniques. Chapter 3 gets down to specifics with end-to-end life cycle processes, activities, tasks, and examples for providing verification and validation of neural networks.

As the demand for developing and assuring adaptive systems grows, this guidebook will provide practitioners with the insight and practical steps for verifying and validating neural networks. The work of the authors is a great step forward, offering a level of practical experience and advice for software developers, assurance personnel, and those performing verification and validation of adaptive systems. This guide makes possible the daunting task of assuring this new technology. NASA is proud to sponsor such a realistic approach to what many might think is a very futuristic subject. But adaptive systems with neural networks are here today and as the NASA Manager for Software Assurance and Safety, I believe this work by the authors will be a great resource for the systems we are building today and into tomorrow.

MARTHA S. WETHERHOLT
NASA Manager of Software Assurance and Software Safety
NASA Headquarters
Office of Safety and Mission Assurance

ACKNOWLEDGMENTS

The authors would like to thank NASA for funding the supporting research that forms the basis of this book. That research was sponsored by NASA Goddard Flight Research Center through the NASA Independent Verification and Validation Facility under Research Grant NAG5-12069. Special thanks goes to Markland Benson, Christina Moats, Ken McGill, Ned Keeler, and Martha Wetherholt for their support and technical comments and suggestions throughout the project. Special mention is also given to NASA Dryden Flight Research Center and NASA Ames Research Center, whose ongoing research in this area was a motivating influence on this work.

Recognition is given to Spiro Skias as project manager for the research project, Kareem Ammar for development of the case studies, Dr. Rebecca Giorcelli for research on hazard and risk analysis, and Stacy Nelson for technical advice during the project.

Special appreciation is given to Dr. Bojan Cukic of West Virginia University. Dr. Cukic and his working group, Sampath Yerramalla and Dr. Edgar Fuller, provided technical direction, support, and suggestions throughout the research project.

LAURA L. PULLUM
EAGAN, MN

BRIAN J. TAYLOR
AMHERST, MA

MARJORIE A. DARRAH
FAIRMONT, WV

December 2006

1

OVERVIEW

Verification is the process of determining whether a system or software is being built correctly. Validation is the process of determining whether a system or software is solving the correct problem. There are several verification and validation (V&V) standards and texts written to address the application of V&V activities on traditional software systems. Traditional software systems are explcitly coded to perform an intended function and do not change behavior or functionality during normal system usage. Most software developed falls within this category.

In contrast to traditional software, adaptive software systems can change behavior, function, internal parameters, or realization while in operation. Adaptive software may be implicitly designed with the final form obtained through optimization techniques, probabilitistic methods, or learning algorithms. Adaptive systems can be implemented with neural networks, genetic algorithms, fuzzy logic, machine learning, expert systems, autonomous planning software, formal logic, or combinations of these and other approaches.

The field of software engineering for adaptive systems is relatively young compared to software engineering for traditional software systems. Traditional software systems have many mature techniques that can be used to understand how they behave. With the uncertainties and complexities associated with adaptive software systems, there is no similar set of mature techniques. Each adaptive system may have its own intrinsic V&V problems and some adaptive software system algorithms are so new that they have never been applied to production or high-assurance projects.

To help address this need, this book contains guidance related to the V&V activities for adaptive software systems. The guidance is based on lessons learned and applied research from development and V&V of a safety- and mission-critical adaptive flight control system. To improve its practicality, the guidance has been written to align with the widely used *IEEE Standard for Software Verification and Validation, IEEE Std 1012-1998* [IEEE 1998].

Mirroring the generalities of some V&V activities, parts of this guidance are applicable to any form of adaptive system. Other parts of this guidance target a subset of adaptive systems, specifically, neural networks. This choice is based on the experience captured from projects that have used adaptive neural network systems and is not an indicator that neural networks are the best choice amongst all possible adaptive systems. Based on this experience, the guidance emphasizes areas for which special consideration should be given when verifying and validating neural networks. In addition, supplemental directives for neural networks were added to the original tasks of IEEE Std 1012, and guidance is also provided for these directives. Even though there is special consideration for neural networks, some of the recommendations are applicable to other types of adaptive software systems.

This guidance is intended for application to adaptive software being developed, maintained, or reused. Software is a key contributor to system behavior and performance. This relationship requires that software V&V processes take software interactions with all system components into consideration. The user of this guidance should consider V&V as a part of the adaptive software life cycle process and not as something done at the end of development. This view of V&V is consistent with IEEE Std 1012 with its provision of V&V processes throughout the (traditional or nontraditional) software life cycle.

1.1   DEFINITIONS AND CONVENTIONS

From IEEE Std 1012, the following definitions are provided:

Verification: (A) The process of evaluating a system or component to determine whether the products of a given development phase satisfy the conditions imposed at the start of that phase. (B) The process of providing objective evidence that the software and its associated products conform to requirements (e.g., for correctness, completeness, consistency, accuracy) for all life cycle activities during each life cycle process (acquisition, supply, development, operation, and maintenance); satisfy standards, practices, and conventions during life cycle processes; and successfully complete each life cycle activity and satisfy all the criteria for initiating succeeding life cycle activities (e.g., building the software correctly).

Validation: (A) The process of evaluating a system or component during or at the end of the development process to determine whether it satisfies specified requirements. (B) The process of providing evidence that the software and its associated products satisfy system requirements allocated to software at the end of each life cycle activity, solve the right problem (e.g., correctly model physical laws, implement business rules, use the proper system assumptions), and satisfy intended use and user needs.

Within this book, the V&V practitioner is simply referred to as the "practitioner." Any person responsible for the design, training, and implementation of the adaptive system is referred to as the "developer" or "designer". Any person responsible for the testing of the adaptive system is referred to as the "tester."

1.2   ORGANIZATION OF THE BOOK

This book aligns with IEEE Std 1012. The alignment will allow the practitioner the ability to quickly reference information on specific areas of interest. This book is organized into three chapters. Chapter 1 provides an introduction and overview of the book. Chapter 2 provides a summary of areas of consideration when using adaptive systems/neural networks. Chapter 3 is the most important chapter and gives the detailed, specific guidance for all life cycle processes, activities, and tasks related to adaptive systems/neural networks. Chapter 3 is organized such that the reader can easily map between the guidance provided and the IEEE standard. Chapter 4 provides a look at the recent update to the standard, IEEE Std 1012-2004, and how updates to the standard impact the practitioner using the guidance provided in this book. Appendices provide lists of references cited, acronyms used, and definitions of terms used throughout the book.

2

AREAS OF CONSIDERATION FOR ADAPTIVE SYSTEMS

When including an adaptive component within a software system, there are several areas that need special consideration, including:

- safety-critical adaptive systems requiring special attention to prevent harm to humans or the environment,
- hazard analysis [for example, via fault model and failure modes and effects analysis (FMEA)],
- requirements for adaptive systems including control and knowledge requirements,
- rule extraction to understand neural network knowledge,
- modified life cycle necessary because of the adaptive nature of neural networks,
- operational monitors to ensure safety after deployment,
- testing considerations, including automated test data generators like the Automated Test Trajectory Generator (ATTG),
- training set analysis to understand what knowledge has been given to the neural network,
- stability analysis to establish a mathematical foundation and proof of convergence for the neural network,
- version control of the adaptive system design,
- simulations with varying fidelity for testing the adaptive component and system,
- visualization techniques to aid in adaptive system development and understanding, and appropriate selection and reasoning for use of adaptive systems.

This chapter describes these special areas and provides general V&V strategies.

2.1   SAFETY-CRITICAL ADAPTIVE SYSTEM EXAMPLE AND EXPERIENCE

The Intelligent Flight Control Systems (IFCS) project provides an excellent example of an adaptive system used in a high assurance system. This example will be used throughout the guidance to help clarify and explain the suggestions for new tasks and task modifications. The IFCS project has been a collaborative effort among the NASA Dryden Flight Research Center (DFRC), the NASA Ames Research Center (ARC), Boeing Phantom Works, and the Institute for Scientific Research, Inc. (ISR). The experience gained through involvement with this project provided important lessons and insight into best practices for V&V of neural networks.

The IFCS project has an ongoing goal to develop and flight-demonstrate an intelligent flight control concept that can efficiently identify aircraft stability and control characteristics using neural networks, and utilize this information to optimize aircraft performance in both actual and simulated failure conditions. A secondary goal is to develop the processes to verify and validate neural networks for use in flight-critical applications. The results of this project will be utilized in an overall strategy aimed at advancing neural network flight control technology to new aerospace systems designs, including civil and military aircraft, reusable launch vehicles, uninhabited vehicles, and space vehicles.

The IFCS was first tested in flight on the NASA F-15 Advanced Control Technology for Integrated Vehicles (ACTIVE) aircraft. This aircraft, shown in Figure 1, was highly modified from a standard F-15 configuration to include canard control surfaces, thrust vectoring nozzles, and a digital fly-by-wire flight control system. The use of canard surfaces along with simulated *stuck* stabilator deflections allows the IFCS project to simulate different actuator failures during flight.

Figure 1. NASA F-15 ACTIVE Aircraft

Two types of neural networks make up the components of the first generation (GEN1) intelligent flight control scheme. A pretrained neural network (PTNN) component provides the baseline approximation of the stability and control derivatives of the aircraft. This neural network is composed of 34 separate multilayer perceptrons, with some of the network's outputs combined to form the derivatives.

The second neural network integrated into the GEN1 intelligent flight control system is a self-organizing map (SOM) neural network, designed by NASA ARC, named Dynamic Cell Structure (DCS). Flight tests of the online learning network will demonstrate a flight control mode for a damaged fighter or transport aircraft that can return the aircraft safely to base.

The second phase of the intelligent flight controller, known as GEN2, made use of a higher-order neural network known as Sigma-Pi. Early designs of GEN2 included another neural network design that was to be used as a competing design against Sigma-Pi. This neural network was a single layer multilayer perceptron (MLP) and internally known as the single-hidden layer (SHL). SHL was ultimately not selected for the GEN2 designs, but preliminary V&V considerations were conducted for it.

Instead of providing support for flight control, these adaptive neural networks are actually a component of the controller. By moving from support to a component of control, GEN2 takes an iterative step of placing the neural network into a higher safety-critical role with the goal of improvements in the flight controller over GEN1. This methodical inclusion of neural network technologies into higher safety- and mission-critical roles is a roadmap planned by both NASA DFRC and NASA ARC.

As high assurance systems, the flight control designs from the IFCS project offer an opportunity to provide examples to V&V practitioners who must deal with adaptive software. Throughout this book, the four neural networks found in the IFCS generation designs, the PTNN, DCS, Sigma-Pi, and SHL, are frequently used in examples. For additional background information on each of these neural networks, and more in-depth description of the IFCS project, the reader can consult [Jorgensen 1997, Calise 2000, NASA DFRC 2004].

2.2   HAZARD ANALYSIS

Hazard analysis is an activity often tailored to a system's software criticality and the potential impact the software has upon overall system risk. Because hazard analysis will vary from project to project, this guidance will assume that hazard analysis tasks occur in the V&V activities, as illustrated in Table 1.

Table 1. Hazard Analysis Tasks Associated with V&V Activities

Concept V&V Activity	Requirements V&V Activity	Design V&V Activity	Implementation V&V Activity	Testing V&V Activity
Preliminary Hazard List Preliminary Hazard Analysis	Software Requirements Hazard Analysis	Software Design Hazard Analysis	Software Code Hazard Analysis	Software Safety Testing Software User Interface Analysis

Several different techniques can be used during software requirements hazard analysis. This section will outline an example that begins by developing a top-level fault model of the neural network. The fault model can then be used to provide a foundation for hazard analysis and risk assessment methods such as hazards and operability studies (HAZOPs), FMEA, and fault tree analysis (FTA). The practitioner will undoubtedly encounter unique software systems, but this example may be useful in identifying common neural network concerns.

2.2.1   Development of a Neural Network Fault Model

One of the simplest types of neural networks is the MLP. MLPs consist of nodes (perceptrons) and connections between them. The nodes contain activation functions that determine the value the node is to assume. The simplest activation function is a step function, one that associates the perceptron with the value one (or zero) if the weighted sum of its inputs exceeds certain threshold value. The weights are associated with all connections. They are adjusted dynamically in training so that the overall learning error is minimized.

An abstract definition of the neural network reveals parameters that could contain faults during both training and operation phases. Together with parameter definitions, based on Bolt's work on neural network fault tolerance [Bolt 1992], network parameters can be associated with potential failures, as shown below:

- *Weights*, w_{ij}, can fail in the operational phase as well as during the training phase. The weights change dynamically while the network is in training mode, whereas they assume fixed values in the operational phase.
- *Threshold Functions*, f_i, are associated with each perceptron. A fault in a threshold function will alter the value associated with a perceptron in some manner. This can affect both training and operational phases.
- *Derivative of Threshold Functions*, f_i', are used to track the change in the activation values of each perceptron. The fault in f_i' will affect the system only during the training phase. It is identified as a separate fault since its impact is generally different from that of f_i.
- *Constant Values* are faults affecting any constant values and are fixed by definition. An example of a constant value in the training phase is the learning rate, η.
- *Target Values*, t_i, represent the function that the neural network attempts to approximate. These values may not be constant since it is conceivable that a MLP network may be trained on data that is modified as time progresses; see, for example, [Miikkulainen 1988].
- *Topology* is the connectivity of the neural network and could easily be subject to faults in various ways, such as the loss of a connection between two units.

There are some additional entities that must be considered for inclusion in the fault model because of their functional role in MLP neural network operation, even though their lifetime is strictly limited. For example, so-called delta values, δ_i, have to be saved while the network is in the training mode so that approximation errors can be evaluated at each pass of the training algorithm. These additional entities are noted below and are derived from Bolt [1992]:

- *Activation Values,* $a_i = \sum_j w_{ij} o_j$

- *Delta,* δ_i – faults in these are only relevant during the training phase.
- *Weight Change,* Δw_{ij} – these are the set of alterations for the stable weight base values, and as for δ_i, faults are only applicable during the training phase.

From the fault model, it can be seen that a large number of possible fault locations exist for a MLP neural network. However, when the fault manifestations are defined, experience has shown that many of them can be omitted from consideration.

The mathematical equations that guide training and operation of MLP neural network are presented in Figure 2.

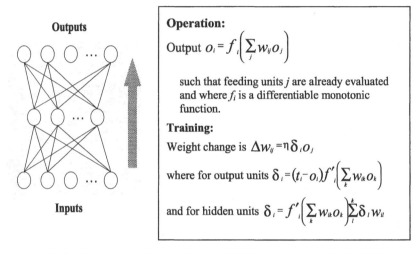

Figure 2. Training and Operation of a Multilayer Perceptron [Bolt 1992]

After identifying entities that may contain faults, the next step is to describe the nature of these faults. To do this, one can use the technique for defining fault manifestations described by Bolt [1992]. First, possible faults are defined using the maximization-of-damage principle, which tends to lead to the discovery of extreme fault modes. The second step using information derived from implementation considerations is then applied to the fault modes. This has the effect of either restricting a mode's effect or ruling it out completely as impossible or irrelevant. A set of failure modes for the MLP neural network is defined by applying these concepts to the fault model (Figure 3).

The next step is to use the information on failure modes above and illustrate its use in performing a FMEA. This requires a sample system and for these purposes the IFCS GEN2 MLP neural network is used (see Table 2). Note that the purpose of the IFCS neural network is to reduce system error.

Weights, w_{ij}

$w_{ij} = 0$ causes loss of any partial information that the weight held

$w_{ij} \rightarrow - w_{ij}$ weight is multiplied by –1; represents a unit always trying to misclassify an input

OR a saturation limit can be applied on any faulty weight by restricting weights to the range $[-W, +W]$. This suggests the faults:

negative $w_{ij} \rightarrow +W$

positive $w_{ij} \rightarrow -W$

Threshold Function

Stuck-at-minus-one

Stuck-at-plus-one

Derivative of Threshold Function

Stuck-at-plus-one

Stuck-at-zero

Learning Rate

$\eta = 0$ typical range $(0, 1]$

η = its highest possible value

Target Values

t_i = value opposite to the fault-free value (the targets generally take only the two values at the extreme ends of the threshold function range)

Topology

Loss of a connection between 2 units

Random reconnection of a link to another unit in the network (possibly due to a short-circuit)

Activation Values, a_i, and Delta, δ_i

Limit to opposite value   OR

Constrain δ_i and a_i to a limited range or randomize them

Weight Change, Δw_{ij}
Only need to be considered if they are stored temporarily, then they would have similar failure modes as those for activation values and deltas

Figure 3. Failure Modes for MLP Neural Networks

Table 2. FMEA for IFCS GEN2 Neural Network

Neural Network Entity	Failure Modes	Local Effect	System Effect
Weights	$w_{ij} = 0$	Incorrect error reduction	Poor handling qualities (HQ); system will compensate, but take longer to compensate than without error.
	$w_{ij} \rightarrow -w_{ij}$	Network instability; unable to converge	System instability; may lose error compensation (LEC) totally. May never regain good flying quality.
Threshold Function (sigmoidal)	Stuck-at-minus-one	Network instability; unable to converge	Poor HQ
	Stuck-at-plus-one	Network instability; unable to converge	Poor HQ
Derivative of Threshold Function	Stuck-at-plus-one	Loss of error fitting (sigmoid becomes linear)	none
	Stuck-at-zero	No error compensation	Poor HQ
Learning Rate	$\eta = 0$ typical range (0, 1]	No weight change, cannot accommodate system error	Poor HQ
	η = its highest possible value	Instability, network unable to achieve local minima (most likely)	LEC
Target Values	t_i = value opposite to the fault-free value (the targets generally take only the two values at the extreme ends of the threshold function range)	Network would move away from optimum error reduction, become more erroneous	LEC
Topology

Topology (continued) | Loss of a connection between 2 units | Incorrect error reduction; loss of internal knowledge | LEC, transient |
	Random reconnection of a link to another unit in the network (possibly due to a short circuit)	Incorrect error reduction; loss of internal knowledge	LEC, transient
Activation Values	Limit to opposite value	Weights adjust in opposite direction $\rightarrow$ double error	Poor HQ
Delta	Limit to opposite value	Weights change in the wrong direction	Poor HQ, transient
Weight Change	Limit to opposite value (Consider only if they are stored temporarily)	Takes longer to converge	Poor HQ

In the context of the sample application discussed above (NASA IFCS GEN2), when the neural network interferes with the proportional-integral derivative (PID) error compensation, the resulting system effect is poorer flying quality than with dynamic inversion alone. There are various ranges of flight quality problems based upon the Cooper-Harper handling qualities scale, e.g., 1-3 is acceptable; 4-6 there is a problem in the system and the system requires some pilot compensation; and 7-8 the pilot must provide considerable compensation to the system. If the neural network failure mode is transient, then the system effect is most likely in the 4-6 range. If the neural network failure mode is permanent, then the system effect can go to the 7-8 range. The table above notes the worst case hazards and assumes no operational monitor or other non-PID combination for fault mitigation.

The bottom-up approach for the FMEA as applied to the IFCS GEN2 Neural Network is presented in Table 2 from left to right. Reading Table 2 from right to left would represent a top-down approach, such as that used for a HAZOP. Essentially, this procedure involves reviewing a full description of a process and systematically questioning every part of it to establish how deviations from the design intent can occur. Once identified, an assessment is made as to whether such deviations and their consequences can have a negative effect upon the safe and efficient operation of the system. If considered necessary, risk mitigation techniques are employed.

This critical analysis is applied in a structured way by the development team. To a large extent, the success of the hazard analysis procedure is dependent upon the knowledge and experience of the team and the ability to release their imagination in an effort to discover credible causes of deviations. In practice, many of the causes will be fairly obvious, such as incorrect knowledge acquisition due to inappropriate training data sets. However, the great advantage of the technique is that it encourages the team to consider less obvious ways in which a deviation may occur, however unlikely they may seem at first consideration. In this way, the study becomes much more than a mechanistic checklist type of review. The result is a higher probability that previously unanticipated potential failures and problems will be identified upfront.

2.3   REQUIREMENTS FOR ADAPTIVE SYSTEMS

Requirements for adaptive systems are difficult to write because the system changes during training and operation. Thus, the initial requirements for an adaptive system may be intentionally incomplete (hence the need to include an adaptive system). The requirements should address the two aspects of the system shown in Figure 4.

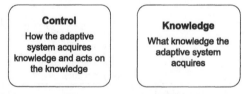

Figure 4. Requirements for Adaptive Systems

The *control*-type requirements are ones that would be typically generated for any software system. The *knowledge*-type requirements are more difficult to write and must fully address the adaptive nature of the system and how it can evolve over time.

Early in the process of developing adaptive system requirements, the adaptive behavior must be clearly defined and documented. Project documents at early stages should contain ***high-level goals*** for the adaptive system behavior and knowledge. The high-level goals are a representation of the problem to be solved, possibly in the form of informal descriptions. These goals stated in early documents, such as the Project Plan, should then be traceable through Systems Requirements, Software and Interface Requirements, and Design documents.

From the high-level goals, the system-level requirements can be developed. One approach to developing requirements related to knowledge in neural networks, and other adaptive systems, may be to model, or describe the knowledge to be acquired in the form of rules [Kurd 2003]. Kurd's model for a Safety Life Cycle is summarized in Section 2.5. Experts or those involved in development can translate knowledge requirements into symbolic rules labeled as ***initial knowledge***.

In Figure 5, the second row of boxes shows how this initial knowledge can lead to refined knowledge as the system is trained and then either to intermediate knowledge given to the adaptive system before deployment or final knowledge if the system is fixed. The top row shows the typical requirements developed for the system. These two rows represent the difference between the control- and knowledge-type requirements. This idea will be revisited in detail during the discussion of several of the life cycle tasks and activities.

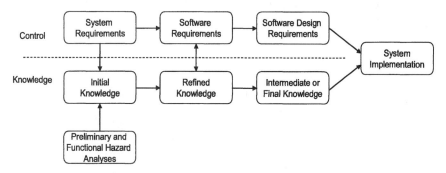

Figure 5. Requirements for Adaptive Systems (Control and Knowledge)

2.4   RULE EXTRACTION

This section offers solutions to the problem of traceability for the knowledge and requirements related to the knowledge of adaptive systems. The information in this section attempts to answer the following questions:

- What is rule extraction? (overview, rule formats and definitions)
- How is rule extraction useful for V&V? (using rule extraction throughout the life cycle, advantages and disadvantages)

2.4.1   What is Rule Extraction?

Rule extraction is the process of developing English-like syntax that describes the internal knowledge of a neural network. Most rule extraction techniques share a common prepositional "if ... then" format. For an extensive review of these techniques and their use for V&V, refer to the following documents [Andrews 1995, Tickle 1998, ISR 2002,

Taylor 2005, Darrah 2004, Kurd 2003]. The same techniques used to map rules from the network in rule extraction can also be used in two additional ways: rule initialization and rule insertion.

Rule initialization is the process of giving the adaptive network some pre-operational knowledge, possibly through early training or configuration. Rule insertion is the method of moving symbolic rules back into a network, forcing the network's knowledge to incorporate some rule modifications or additional rules.

2.4.2   Rule Formats and Definitions

Rule extraction algorithms can generate rules of either conjunctive form or subset selection form, commonly referred to as M-of-N rules named for the primary rule extraction technique that makes use of the subset selection form. All rules follow the logical syntax of an if-then prepositional form. Conjunctive rules follow the format shown in Figure 6.

IF condition 1 AND condition 2 AND condition 3 THEN *RESULT*

Figure 6. Example of Conjunctive Rules

Here the RESULT can be of a binary value (TRUE/FALSE or YES/NO), a classification value (e.g., RED/WHITE/BLUE), a real number value (e.g., 0.18), or a functional expression of the inputs.

The condition can be either discrete (e.g., flower is RED, ORANGE, or YELLOW) or continuous (e.g., $0.25 \leq$ diameter ≤ 0.6). The rule extraction algorithm will search through the structure of the network and/or the contents of a network's training data and narrow down values across each input, looking for the antecedents (conditions) that make up the rules. Subset rules, or M-of-N rules, follow the format shown in Figure 7.

IF (M of the following N antecedents are TRUE) THEN *RESULT*

Figure 7. Example of Subset Rules

Cravin and Shavlik explain that the M-of-N rule format provides more concise rule sets in contrast to the potentially lengthy conjunctive rule format [Craven 1994]. This can be especially true when a network uses several input parameters and a value for several of these parameters composes the rule.

2.4.3   Types of Rule Extraction

Rule extraction techniques can primarily be classified into one of three categories: decompositional, pedagogical, and eclectic.

Decompositional rule extraction involves the extraction of rules from a network in a neuron-by-neuron series of steps. This process can be tedious and results in large and complex descriptions. The drawbacks to decompositional extractions are time and computational limitations. The advantages of decompositional techniques are that they seem to offer the prospect of generating a complete set of rules for the neural network.

Pedagogical rule extraction is the extraction of a network description by treating the entire network as a black box. In this approach, inputs and outputs are matched to each other. The decompositional approaches can produce intermediary rules that are defined for internal connections of a network. Pedagogical approaches usually do not result in these intermediary terms. Pedagogical approaches can be faster than decompositional approaches, but they are somewhat less likely to accurately capture all of the valid rules describing a network's contents.

The *eclectic* approach is merely the use of those techniques that incorporate some aspects of a decompositional approach with some aspects of a pedagogical approach, or techniques designed in such a way that they can be either decompositional or pedagogical.

2.4.4   How is Rule Extraction Useful in V&V?

Rule extraction, rule initialization, and rule insertion can all be used for V&V purposes throughout the development life cycle. During the Concept, Requirements, Design, Implementation, and Testing Activities, different aspects of these techniques can be applied. Kurd, Kelly, and Austin [2003] describe a model that uses rule initialization, extraction, and insertion and ties the hazard analysis into the development of the neural networks' knowledge. The model is described in Section 2.5.2.

Rule extraction offers the possibility of requirements traceability throughout the entire development life cycle. Requirements for adaptive systems are difficult to write because the system changes during training and operation, as explained in Section 2.3. The rule extraction process can help guide requirements writing, with the requirements for knowledge being written in a format that can be compared to the rules. The requirements can then be used as assertions that are tested against the rules extracted from trained neural networks.

The extracted rules can also undergo design team review and analysis to detect improper network behaviors or missing knowledge. A system analyst might be able to ascertain novel learning behaviors that had not been previously recognized. By translating these features into comprehensible logical statements, the analyst can gain not only a better understanding of the network internal knowledge, but, potentially, the input domain as well.

Rule insertion can be used to apply a condition within the network or reinforce conditions already existing in the network. Examples of this include restricting the network to a region of the input space or instructing it to deliberately forget some data it has already seen. Rules that translate system hazards or requirements can also be inserted into the network [Kurd 2003].

2.4.5   Advantages and Disadvantages

Rule extraction from neural networks may have greater utility for fixed neural networks than for dynamic neural networks. Fixed neural networks proceed through the steps of training and testing until they reach an acceptable error threshold and only then are they used within a system. The knowledge of the domain is considered to be embedded inside the weights and connections of the network. If the network is no longer encouraged to adapt, the symbolic rules extracted to describe it can be a useful tool to validate that network at the time of extraction.

With a dynamic neural network, symbolic rule extraction may be required at intermediate stages in the learning. At some intermediate points, symbolic rules would need to be extracted and passed through an oracle or system monitor to confirm that the network was still "correct." The maximum benefits for dynamic systems may lie with rule insertion or rule initialization.

2.5   MODIFIED LIFE CYCLE FOR DEVELOPING NEURAL NETWORKS

The traditional software development life cycle does not adequately address the development of adaptive systems, specifically, neural networks. The first reason that the traditional methods do not work is that "one does not really write code for neural networks" [Rodvold 1999]. Neural networks are formed as they are trained or in realtime as they adapt. The second reason that neural networks need to be treated differently is that the risks associated with neural networks are heavily tied to the development activity. Two ideas are presented in this section that relate specifically to a modified development life cycle for neural network development.

2.5.1   Nested Loop Model of Neural Network Development Process

The following information is summarized from "A Software Development Process Model for Artificial Neural Networks in Critical Applications," written by David M. Rodvold [1999]. Rodvold suggests a Nested Loop Model for neural network development as depicted in Figure 8. This model combines two commonly used software development models: the waterfall model and some aspects of the spiral model. The model includes five steps that are briefly described below. The steps proceed from the upper-left corner of the figure to the lower-right corner.

Step 1: Network Requirements, Goals, and Constraints. This task develops the *Network Performance Specifications.* This document is a downsized version of the System Requirement Specification and contains specific neural network requirements, goals, and constraints.

Step 2: Data Gathering and Preprocessing. This task involves assembling the data to be used for training the neural network. All activities associated with the data preparation should be recorded, including data sources, original format of data, modifications performed on data, and any information about the pedigree or fidelity of the data that is available. The preprocessing at this point is to collect the data into a format that the training package can use. This task should result in a *Data Analysis Document* that provides traceability for the training database.

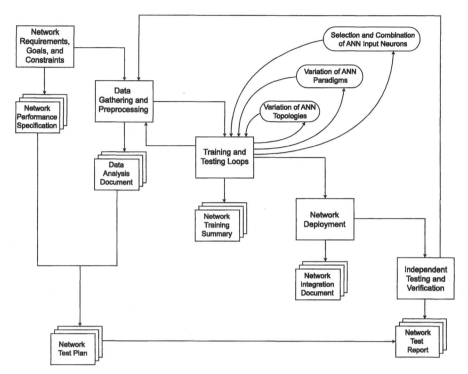

Figure 8. Nested Loop Model of Neural Network Development Process [Rodvold 1999]

Step 3: Training and Testing Loops. The Training and Testing Loops represent an iterative process in which the neural network architecture is developed and trained. The innermost loop, Variations of ANN (artificial neural network) Topologies, denotes the changes of the architectural parameters. For example, for multilayer perceptrons this may include variations in the number of hidden layers, neurons per layer, activation function choices, biases on the neuron connections, and similar parameters.

In the middle loop, Variations of ANN Paradigms, the developer may experiment with the type of neural network used. The outer loop, Selection and Combination of ANN Input Neurons, focuses on the inputs that the neural network is to model. This loop involves choosing the proper subset of inputs to best model the domain and deciding what preprocessing of inputs is required.

During this task, the developer should examine the training set for completeness and make sure that the problem is completely specified by the input parameters. The activities preformed during the training process should be documented in the *Network Training Summary*. This document should include a complete list of all permutations that were tried, along with the results achieved. All input data files used should be attached electronically.

Step 4: Network Deployment. There are three general ways by which Network Deployment is performed. First, many commercial tools include runtime libraries that can be linked to the trained network file. The second method is automatic code generation facilities provided by commercial tools. Third, the developers can save raw network data to a text file. In the latter case, the developer must write or otherwise acquire the code to load the neural network data and exercise the network.

In any of these cases, the developer should document the deployment effort and record all manually or automatically generated source code in the *Network Integration Document.*

Step 5: Independent Testing and Verification. The first task of the testing group is to construct the *Network Test Plan,* based on the *Network Performance Specifications* and the *Data Analysis Document.* The test plan should include a critical review of all phases of the development effort including: data gathering, training database, preprocessing, and deployment. The testing group should include summaries of all tests performed and electronic copies of test programs or databases in the *Network Test Report.*

2.5.2   Safety Life Cycle for Hybrid Neural Networks

The following information is summarized from "Safety Criteria and Safety Life Cycle for Artificial Neural Networks," written by Kurd, Kelly, and Austin [2003]. The authors describe a process for developing neural networks considering the criteria that must be enforced to justify the safety of the neural network in operation. This model ties the hazard analysis to the development of the neural network's knowledge and specifically addresses neural networks developed for safety-critical applications.

Figure 9 illustrates the development and safety life cycle. The three main levels and the major stages in the diagram are described below.

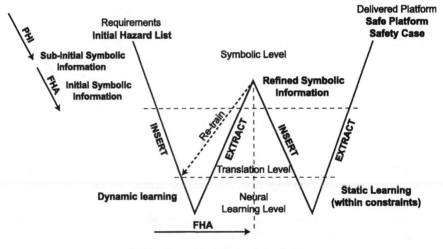

FHA: Functional Hazard Analysis
PHI: Preliminary Hazard Identification

Figure 9. Safety Lifecycle for Hybrid Neural Networks [Kurd 2003]

The three major levels in the diagram are Symbolic Level, Translation Level, and Neural Learning Level. The Symbolic Level is associated with the symbolic information. At this level, the gathering and processing of initial knowledge occurs, as well as evaluating extracted knowledge gathered after learning. The Translation Level is where the symbolic knowledge and the neural architectures are combined or separated through the use of rule insertion and rule extraction techniques. The Neural Learning Level uses neural learning to refine the symbolic knowledge through the training of the neural network, using learning algorithms.

The major stages that outline the process follow the "W" model in the development life cycle. These stages are:

- *Determination of requirements* – These requirements describe the problem to be solved in informal terms and are intentionally incomplete.
- *Subinitial knowledge* – Knowledge (given by domain experts) is translated into logical rules.
- *Initial knowledge* – The rules that describe the subinitial knowledge are converted into symbolic forms compatible for translation into the neural network structure.
- *Dynamic learning* – Suitable learning algorithms and training sets are used to refine the initial symbolic knowledge and add new rules to reduce the error in the output. This may result in topological changes to the neural network.
- *Refined symbolic knowledge* – Knowledge refined by the learning is extracted using appropriate algorithms. This results in a new set of rules that can be analyzed.
- *Static learning* – Refined symbolic knowledge may be modified by domain experts and re-inserted into the neural network. This further refines the knowledge in the neural network but does not allow topological or architectural changes.
- *Knowledge extraction* – This can be performed at any time during static learning to get a modified rule set.

2.6   OPERATIONAL MONITORS

Online adaptation creates unique problems for V&V. The system is adapting itself in realtime and thus each input may cause internal adjustments. Technically, these adjustments to the system would require testing to see if the modifications still allow the system to meet the set requirements. Testing at any particular point in time only "proves" the system for that moment; the next data input, whether valid or not, has the potential to alter the behavior of the system as it adapts to accommodate the new information into its behavior. Therefore, constant or periodic verification and validation must be performed to detect system anomalies before a catastrophic event can occur.

Operational monitoring involves evaluating the adaptive software component during operation, and/or evaluating information such as event logs collected from its execution. Generally, this requires a secondary application that runs concurrently with the target application. The operational monitoring program records specified information (such as data value and time stamp) for selected variables and events. The information collected can be used to detect violations of system constraints or to manage resources at runtime.

There are different operational monitoring approaches. One approach, "data sniffing," evaluates the validity of the input and output and helps assess and control the adaptive reasoning process of the program. This method utilizes a prealert agent and postblock agent to assess the target program [Lui 2002]. The prealert agent captures the incoming data before it enters the system and determines whether or not it may cause unexpected (undesired) adaptations in the system. If so, it offers a warning and allows the data into the system with caution. The postblock agent examines the postclassification value, determines its "distance" to training class norms, and, should the new value fall well outside the training domain, prevents it from being used.

Another example of an operational monitoring approach is utilized in the Sensitivity Tool used for an adaptive intelligent flight control system [Soares 2002]. This approach uses Lyapunov's Second Method for stability analysis of a neural network-based flight control system. The tool tracks error and network weights to determine if the signal remains bounded and exercises the gain sensitivity to determine changes in the weights and the inversion errors. The tool can also add white noise to the neural network in order to determine the sensitivity of the flight control model to varying levels of noise. The user interface of the Sensitivity Tool can display MATLAB plots depicting information such as neural network error and neural network weight trajectory. This allows the user to visually see the progress of the neural network during operation.

The Confidence Tool is another operational monitoring device [Gupta 2004]. This tool measures the performance of the neural network in operation by calculating a confidence interval around the neural network output. For the approach used by the Confidence Tool, only one scalar value per neural network needs to be recorded. IFCS GEN2 includes the confidence tool within the research system. As there is a neural network for each of the longitudinal, lateral, and directional axes, three confidence values are available for telemetry during runtime and are recorded in local memory for later inspection.

A comprehensive approach to operational monitoring is taken by Cukic et al. in [Taylor 2005]. Their approach combines several different techniques into a four-monitor system. Each monitor observes a different aspect of the system. The information is brought together to give an overall rating for the confidence in the adaptive system. This comprehensive approach is important because some projects may not be satisfied with monitoring a single aspect of the neural network for run-time V&V of a safety- or a mission-critical system.

The NN (Neural Network) Evaluator is another example of an operational monitor that examines several aspects of a neural network [ISR 2004]. This operational monitor evaluates irregular behavior of the Sigma-Pi neural networks in IFCS GEN2. The goal of NN Evaluator is to alert human operators when monitored fault indicators exceed predetermined decision thresholds. The fault indicators evaluate the neural network through criteria such as weight changes and Lyapunov functions. The decision thresholds are determined through simulations and verified by flight tests.

2.7   TESTING CONSIDERATIONS

The testing of the neural network design and implementation centers around four important areas: the neural network interface, the implementation of the underlying functions, the acquired knowledge, and the internal structure. A representation of these areas is shown in Figure 10.

These four areas are used throughout the guidance's discussion on test planning, test design, test case generation, and test procedure generation. The areas of knowledge, function, and structure testing are found within component testing, whereas the area of interface testing is found in integration, even though it, too, can be performed in component-level testing.

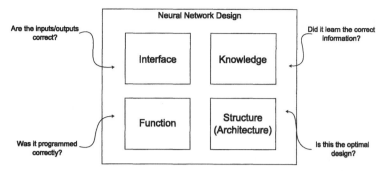

Figure 10. Areas to Test in Neural Network Design and Implementation

Throughout this guidance, five different methods are identified that can be used during the testing of a neural network system. These are traditional training-testing approach, automated test generation, guided by stability proofs, guided by operational monitoring design, and guided by rule extraction. Further discussion on each of these methods is provided in this chapter.

2.7.1 Interface Testing

Interface testing should be concerned with evaluating the inputs and outputs of the neural network and how the network receives and transmits these to other modules within the system. This testing needs to ensure that the inputs are sent into the neural network in a correct order by those modules creating the inputs. The interface inside the neural network will need to be tested as well to ensure that the network receives these inputs in a correct order. Likewise, the outputs of the neural network need to be verified for proper order. Other aspects of this testing will evaluate if proper preprocessing and postprocessing occur within the neural network module, and if the input and output units/dimensions are correct.

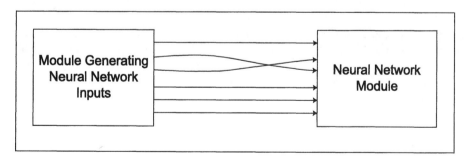

Figure 11. Illustration of an Input Order Switch

The importance of testing the interfacing details, even by inspection of the code, is because neural networks can be quite robust during learning and are able to mask incorrect inputs. It is possible that two inputs can be switched (from a sending module to the neural network inputs). If these two signals have similar magnitudes, the neural network may be able to approach highly accurate results during a test run and later demonstrate poor performance with different inputs.

2.7.2   Function Testing

Function testing is no different for a neural network than it is for any other type of software. Nonetheless, it is an area that the practitioner should ensure undergoes testing. Aspects of function testing include testing the implementation of the underlying functions of the neural network. The functions to be tested include, but are not limited to, the activation functions, transfer functions, learning algorithms, and growing algorithms.

As many of these functions are mathematical in nature, testing should ensure that all functions produce acceptable values for desired ranges.   Some functions may be implemented as lookup tables or approximated through simplified algorithms. These should be checked for correctness throughout the entire range lest numerical inconsistencies exist anywhere within the range, especially for boundary conditions.

2.7.3   Knowledge Testing

Knowledge testing is perhaps the most difficult area of neural network analysis because it involves evaluating if the neural network is learning what the designers want it to learn. The problem is that it may be difficult to understand the internal knowledge, and the practitioner must use means other than those offered through standard testing.

Traditionally, knowledge testing is accomplished through testing the neural network on a small amount of data that was never used to provide network training. This is the training-testing approach often mentioned in neural network texts. Anywhere from 20-25% of the original data available to a project is used for testing purposes to determine if the neural network knowledge gained from learning on the other 75-80% is adequate.

As this guidance book explains in several sections, the traditional training-testing approach may not provide enough assurance of correctness. Using a sample of the original data may not allow enough variance to represent real-world data to provide confidence in the testing results. Suggestions made throughout the guidance provided herein center around rule extraction and the translation of the internal neural network knowledge into a set of symbolic rules. The rules are then easier to understand and verify than the standard neural network descriptions that include weights and connections. Another suggestion is the ATTG or approaches similar to the ATTG mentioned within Neural Network Testing Tools below.

2.7.4   Structure Testing

The analysis of the neural network structure evaluates if the neural network architecture is an optimal solution to the problem. Since there are a limitless number of design options for a neural network (including architecture selection, number of neurons, number of internal layers, initial weight selections, function selection, input selection, etc.), the objective of structure testing is to determine if the current design works as well, if not better, than other approaches. Another way to consider this form of testing is the verification that the current design is better than previous designs of the system.

If a formal proof of correctness is provided, that may be all a practitioner requires. Another option is to track the design process of the neural network in a version control system and demonstrate that over time the neural network metrics showed improvement. These metrics include output error, response times, and size of the training set that the neural network can correctly handle. Design alterations come in the form of changes in the number of internal layers of the neural network, changes in the number of neurons within each layer, changes to the learning/growing functions, and others. With each of these changes, the developers must test the neural network performance and track these results.

Because of the vast number of possibilities, it will be nearly impossible for the practitioner to ensure that the current design is the best of all possible designs. Instead the practitioner should look at the design changes and ensure that there are reasons based on performance that support that the current design should be considered better than other alternatives.

2.7.5   Neural Network Testing Tools

Automated test data generation is not a new technique. However, the use of test data generation techniques with neural networks has only recently been investigated [Taylor 1999]. The details the ATTG tool developed by Taylor are given in [Taylor 2005]. Essentially, this tool models relationships within the available test data that are then used to create additional, statistically related data. The tool is used to model continuous time-series data.

Given a set of test data (which can be separated into independent and dependent variables), the ATTG builds a regressive model of the data based upon these independent-dependent relationships. It then uses predefined perturbations to the original independent data to generate new sets of independent and dependent data.

The tool can generate new sets of related data to supplement insufficient test data based upon the user's preferences. It can be used for sensitivity analysis in which newly generated data is used to introduce small variances from the original test data. The ATTG can also facilitate creation of unique or unusual data that may not be contained within the original data set (such as data for testing boundaries or areas within the input domain that may not be exercised sufficiently). The ATTG can also be used to simply expand the existing set of test data to improve test coverage.

The ATTG was created because available testing tools lacked the ability to create sequences of continuous data. Most test data generators deal with single-valued data generation (such as random data generation) or with generating test sets that exercise sequences of code or pathwise coverage. The ATTG, however, can be used to create large amounts of continuous data. For example, the ATTG has been used to create aircraft data such as mach, altitude, angular accelerations, and state space measurements over time. For these reasons, the ATTG is a viable alternative for testing neural networks, especially those within control systems.

2.8   TRAINING SET ANALYSIS

An important step toward gaining an understanding of how the adaptive system may behave is to analyze the selection, construction, and application of the training data that will be used for knowledge. Adaptive systems, specifically neural networks, differ from traditional software programming due to the acquisition of knowledge. Rather than having a specific design that is implemented by a software design, the adaptive system, in a sense, self-programs. The underlying functionality can be programmed and well defined, but the states that the adaptive system can achieve are not known in advance. A possible way to understand what these states might be is through analysis of training data.

Limiting the discussion to neural networks alone still reveals an abundant amount of literature within publications, books, and on the internet on how training sets can be analyzed. Only a few concepts or considerations are presented here.

2.8.1   Training Data with Too Many or Too Few Inputs

If the training data is overly large, the neural network might have a problem learning to the accuracy levels desired by the project. If the goal is generalization, the designers may want to identify the most significant pieces of data from the training set and use those rather than train from too large a set. If the goal is specialization, the designers may want to ensure that all of the data are close, within some defined distance, of each other.

2.8.2   "The Curse of Dimensionality"

If the dimension of the data is too large, then the neural network may have trouble achieving desired accuracies. This is a well-known problem within the neural network literature and several solutions exist, including use of statistical techniques like multivariate analysis or principle component analysis.

2.8.3   Data Redundancy

Data that is redundant within the training set can be interpreted by the neural network as being more significant than other data on average, especially if the redundant data is presented to the network for learning sequentially.

2.8.4   Irrelevant Data

Data that is unlikely to occur during system operation or is insignificant to the project design may need to be removed from the training set. By reducing irrelevant data, the neural network might generalize better or better learn the specific underlying function of the data.

2.8.5 Combining Different Data Sets into One

In some situations, the collection of data to form the training set may come from different sources. The combination of data may not be easy due to differences between the data sets such as noise, sampling rates, or scaling. There can also exist gaps between different data sets that require interpolation. Gaps between the data sets can be acquired by the neural network and mirrored in the knowledge.

2.8.6 Processing the Training Data

The training data may need to undergo processing if the neural network has no preprocessing of its own. Application of smoothing, clustering, and other techniques to the data can have significant effects on the process of learning. Sometimes, such techniques improve learning. Occasionally, they do not.

2.8.7 Data Outliers

Data outliers are pieces of data that have a greater distance from the overall data set than what is found on average, where distance is defined by some criterion like geometry. Removal of data outliers, like removing irrelevant data, can affect learning for the better.

2.8.8 Use of Rule Extraction/Insertion/Refinement with Training Data

One possible means of traceability analysis is the use of a machine learner applied to the original neural network training data to develop rules that describe the training data set. Then, after training of the neural network, a rule extraction algorithm could be used to translate the inner workings of the neural network into a set of rules. A comparison can then be made between one system's statistical interpretation of the data (the machine learning) and the other system's (the neural network).

The uses of rule translations within training extend beyond the possibility of performing traceability. As mentioned in Section 2.5.2, training data can be derived from the conversion of preliminary and functional hazards that are represented as rules. As Figure 9 depicts, this symbolic information can be used in an iterative step during the training process to strengthen the learning of the neural network system.

2.8.9 Training Data and Operational Monitoring

Section 2.6 discusses how training data may be used to construct one form of an operational monitor for an adaptive system. When a neural network is to undergo supervised learning to achieve desired outputs, these same outputs can be used to determine how the network is performing while in use.

2.8.10   Version Control of the Training Process

An often-overlooked consideration in the development of neural networks is the tracking of how the neural network was trained. This includes the data sets used, the order in which they are used, and the frequency with which they are used. In essence, there seems to be a lack of version control for neural network training processes. Without version control, repetition of a specific neural network design could be irreproducible. Section 2.10 discusses some of these issues in depth.

2.9   STABILITY ANALYSIS

A crucial part of the V&V of a neural network system is to establish the mathematical foundation and to provide a proof of convergence for the network. This mathematical approach should be part of the development team's early conceptual work and can also be used as a basis for testing and operational monitoring.

Lyapunov stability analysis can play a critical role in the V&V of neural networks. Lyapunov's Direct (Second) Method is widely used for stability analysis of linear and nonlinear systems, both time invariant and time varying. Viewed as a generalized energy method, it is used to determine if a system is stable, unstable, or marginally stable. A Lyapunov function is an energy-like function of the state variables of the systems and must always be positive, except for equilibrium points where it is equal to zero.

A Lyapunov function has the following properties that can be verified:

- continuous function,
- continuous first order partial derivative over the domain,
- strictly positive except at the equilibrium point,
- zero at the equilibrium point,
- approaches a value of infinity as time moves toward infinity, and
- first difference that is strictly negative in the domain, except at the equilibrium point. [Reed 1999]

The Lyapunov function is not unique; rather, many different Lyapunov functions may be found for a given system. Likewise, the inability to find a satisfactory Lyapunov function does not mean that the system is unstable. There is no universal method for constructing a Lyapunov function. A form of the function can be assumed, either as a pure guess or constructed from physical insight. Consult [Taylor 2005, Yerramalla 2003a, Yerramalla 2003b] for examples of this method.

The formal mathematical descriptions and stability analysis of the neural network should be included in the concept documentation. Software requirements should not be considered complete without reference or inclusion of the stability criteria. During the Design Activity, the stability criteria should help guide the design choices for the neural network, for example, assisting in the validation of any neural network parameter adjustments made during the iterative design process. The stability analysis and operational monitoring may also direct the generation and selection of test procedures and test cases. If the stability criteria have been identified, interesting test points can be within, along, and outside of these stable boundaries. Throughout the Operation Process of the life cycle, stability analysis can play an important role in assessing the health of the system by working as part of an operational monitoring scheme.

2.10 CONFIGURATION MANAGEMENT OF NEURAL NETWORK TRAINING AND DESIGN

Typically, the configuration management process implements version control to track revisions to software and documentation. With adaptive systems, a similar idea can be applied to tracking knowledge revisions by capturing the iterative process of building up knowledge within the adaptive system. Version control of a system acquiring knowledge provides explainability, repeatability, and inspection. It can also be used to remove knowledge by simply repeating a process up to some prior point or extracting an adaptive system out of the version control system after some prior learning point.

Experience indicates that in most non-safety-critical system development, the design and training of a neural network is more of an art form than science. At the end of neural network development, the developers may know they have a neural network that meets some system requirements, but they have no ability to recreate the exact design of the network.

Although this scenario may not be a problem in the non-critical safety domain, software assurance practices may require neural network designs to be explainable and recreatable when safety is a concern. If a neural network is being reused from a previous project, yet no information was captured as to how it was trained or what training data was used, its usefulness to the new project will be severely limited. The practitioner may have reservations about the component's reuse because the project may not be able to explain what knowledge is within the system.

For example, the lack of knowing how a neural network was trained may make further training suboptimal. If all prior training is known and tracked through version control, neural network developers can then determine the optimal training strategy and improve the system design. The order and frequency of a training set application can impact the success of that network in learning the desired concepts. Haphazardly applying training data and not understanding how new learning affects older learning is not acceptable for high-criticality systems.

Items for consideration when tracking the neural network training process are as follows:

- Tracking training data. This may seem trivial, but if the training data used is not tracked within the project, the training data can easily become lost over time. If the training data is modified and not tracked, the exact contents of the training data at any single point in time can be lost. Training data should at least be tracked with a configuration ID and date stamp for each set of data. A set of training data can be defined by the project but could include multiple data files or be completely contained within a single data file. Version or revision identification should be used whenever the training data is modified or updated.
- Tracking the order in which data sets are applied. Tracking the order in which a training set is applied allows for repeatability of the learning. Tools to automatically track the order in which the training data sets are used may not be available. In this case, manual tracking is required.

- Tracking the frequency with which data sets are applied (pass through once, pass through twice, etc.). As with tracking the training set order, this might also require a manual process.
- Tracking the adaptive system after it has been allowed to learn from a training data set. In addition to tracking the order and frequency of applying training data, the adaptive system can be checked into a version control system to store a copy of the adaptive system with its knowledge. This is useful if training is later deemed erroneous and some prior version of the adaptive system with knowledge is needed to continue a different training process.

2.11   SIMULATIONS OF ADAPTIVE SYSTEMS

Modeling and simulations can be integral in the development of an adaptive system and are used extensively in safety-critical applications. Simulations aid in system testing as well as in design and implementation. Low-level fidelity simulations provide the ability for developers to rapidly prototype different neural network architectures early in the life cycle [Taylor 2005]. Moderate-level and major-level fidelity simulations assist in neural network optimization, integration testing, and evaluating operational monitors. High-level fidelity simulations can provide feedback from a human-in-the-loop and offer an environment for acceptance testing.

Table 3 lists fidelity levels used in this book and provides a possible scenario for implementation. Since adaptive systems vary significantly, specific guidance on simulation design is difficult to provide. For that reason, this section offers a few examples of simulations from the IFCS project with implementations and features that may scale to other projects.

Table 3. Fidelity Levels

Fidelity Level	Possible Scenario
Low	Mathematical Model
Moderate	Actual Source Code on a Workstation
Major	Software-in-the-Loop Simulation
High	Hardware-in-the-Loop Simulation or Replication of Target Environment

The IFCS project used several different simulative environments. In the first generation of the IFCS, ISR developed a DCS neural network simulation in MATLAB and Simulink. The MATLAB simulation was considered a very low-fidelity simulation since it did not interface with other system components. ISR also developed a simulation that ran on a Solaris workstation with the target DCS neural network software implemented in the "C" language. This software-in-the-loop simulation (SILS) was considered a moderate-level fidelity simulation because it used the actual target software.

Another example of a low-level fidelity simulation is the IFCS F-15 WVU Simulator [Perhinschi 2002]. This simulation has several helpful features. The graphical user interface (GUI) displays numerous real-time visualizations depicting information such as aircraft flight states, aircraft parameters, and neural-network-related parameters. The

GUI also has the ability to display only information that is pertinent to a specific user. For instance, computer science researchers can display just neural network parameters and error functions when executing the simulator. Additionally, the simulator was designed in a modular fashion. This enables the substitution and comparison of several different adaptive components within the same platform.

In IFCS GEN2, ISR adopted a version of the IFCS F-15 WVU Simulator. The adaptive component in the simulator was removed and was replaced with the target hardware and adaptive software. This setup is considered to be between a moderate-level and major-level fidelity simulation. The target hardware can process the neural network as if it were integrated in the aircraft and supply visual feedback to operators by way of the Simulator's GUI.

The IFCS project also used a piloted hardware-in-the-loop simulator (HILS). The HILS enabled verification of the adaptive system in an integrated closed loop environment with several F-15 components [BPW 2003]. Pilots using this simulation became accustomed to new handling qualities introduced by the adaptive system while engaging in the same maneuvers that would be performed during a flight test. The HILS also permits evaluation of aircraft responses to injected failures from the adaptive component as part of failure modes and effects testing. These failures were mitigated through safety monitors that were also present in the F-15 ACTIVE aircraft.

2.12 NEURAL NETWORK VISUALIZATION

In safety-critical adaptive systems, visualizations are necessary because it is difficult for humans to directly inspect a neural network. Most of the information within a neural network is in the form of real-valued parameters, and there may be thousands of these parameters [Craven 1992]. Further complicating understanding, relational concepts within a neural network are usually distributed across several connected units.

Visualization techniques help in understanding different aspects of a neural network. Chapter 7 of [Taylor 2005] describes several visualization tools and scientific visualization techniques used in neural network development. These visualizations can depict information from neural network architecture, structure, activation functions, training, error functions, input/output (I/O) analysis, and simulations. Also, visualizations can create representations of neural network knowledge or of rules from rule extraction techniques. These can help reveal violations in requirements that may otherwise be difficult to detect.

Visualizations are used throughout the project life cycle. In early life cycle phases, visualizations can depict neural network architecture or structure. These visualizations can help in the development of requirements and in selecting architectures for specific problem domains. During the design phase, environments with visual interfaces, such as MATLAB Neural Network Toolbox, aid in the training process of a neural network. Visualization techniques can illustrate incorrect or abnormal learning and may also lead to undiscovered associations or features within a neural network. When testing an adaptive system, visualizations incorporated into simulative environments can display, in real time, neural network performance. During Operation V&V, visualizations assist in analyzing recorded information from operational monitors, and can even be directly integrated into the operational monitor as in Confidence Tool [Gupta 2004] and Sensitivity Tool [Soares 2002] for real-time analysis.

2.13   ADAPTIVE SYSTEM AND NEURAL NETWORK SELECTION

An important assessment that should be conducted early on in the project is determination of the appropriateness of using an adaptive system or neural network. Neural networks in particular are like multipurpose tools. They generally are used in statistical applications and, because of this, different architectures are usable for different problem types. At best, this section can serve as an initial guide to aid the practitioner in performing this assessment. The best advice is to make sure the project documents why it has made a selection and provides supporting evidence for the selection.

2.13.1   General Adaptive Systems

The information in this section is a summary of ideas from Anderson [1992] and Chapter 4 of *Methods and Procedures for the Verification and Validation of Artificial Neural Networks* [Taylor 2005]. This includes a discussion on the analysis of the problem domain and how the problem/solution classification can lend insight into appropriate use of adaptive systems or neural networks.

The practitioner should ensure that a project making use of an adaptive system is doing so for appropriate reasons. Not only do adaptive systems significantly increase the level of effort needed to assure the system, failure to properly assure an adaptive system can result in severe consequences for safety- and mission-critical systems. The first step toward this evaluation is an understanding of the possible problem-solution combinations.

For this guidance, a problem domain is defined as consisting of the problem and the solution. Each of these problem domains can be classified as either adaptive or fixed, as defined below:

- *Adaptive problem* – a problem that can change over time. Examples of adaptive problems include dynamic operating conditions under which a system must handle unforeseen events or circumstances.
- *Adaptive solution* – a solution that changes over time. Examples of adaptive solutions include situations in which system designers have limited understanding of a problem, and lack the ability to clearly capture and specify the system. For these systems, it is hoped that during operation the system improves the designers' understanding. In this manner, the problem being solved is itself not dynamic, but the solution is dynamic as it adjusts toward a correct answer.
- *Fixed problem* – a problem that is static and will never change. Fixed problems remain the same across time.
- *Fixed solution* – a solution that is static and will never change. Fixed solutions have consistent results and the same input-output mapping for all time.

If the system requirements call for the use of an adaptive system, the practitioner should consider whether an adaptive system is appropriate, given the project goals. There are many reasons an adaptive system may be used, including:

- The problem to be solved is adaptive, and a fixed solution provides limited benefit.
- Adaptation offers a way to improve system performance (this reason should be

proven by documentation).

- Adaptive systems offer a lower production cost or development time without unreasonably raising associated risk.

Figure 12 shows the four categories along with some advice to aid the practitioner in this evaluation.

	Adaptive Solution	Fixed Solution
Adaptive Problem	Pros • can change over time to minimize system error • solution can start with little to no knowledge (initialization) and through learning the problem may lead to better problem understanding Cons • carries higher risk since system will change after deployment • may require additional computational resources	Pros • carries lower risk since solution is known prior to system deployment • if of traditional design, can be more easily verified and validated Cons • non-adaptive solution can lead to varying system error as the problem changes
Fixed Problem	Pros • useful for domains in which the problem is too complex to define for standard programming techniques Cons • carries higher risk since system will change after deployment • may require additional computational resources	Pros • carries lower risk since solution is known prior to system deployment • if of traditional design, can be more easily verified and validated Cons • if the problem domain is too difficult to be well-defined through mathematical/logical representation, then the fixed solution may not be useful

Figure 12. Problem Domain Classification

It should be noted that adaptive solutions can be trained to some acceptable state and then no longer allowed to adapt. This effectively turns the solution into a fixed solution. Because fixed solutions carry a reduced amount of risk, the project may start with an adaptive solution, and plans made to hold it fixed after some acceptable level of change.

2.13.2 Neural Network Systems at a High Level

Because it is impossible to foretell the type of problems for which a neural network may be proposed, a little guidance is presented here to aid the practitioner. This high-level discussion will address the appropriateness of a neural network solution abstractly (vs. mathematically).

The characteristic of a complete solution or an incomplete solution is the most influential factor in deciding the appropriateness of a neural network for a project. A *complete solution* is one that can correctly operate given any input from within the possible input space. A solution that computes integer arithmetic is complete. An abstract representation is shown in Figure 13.

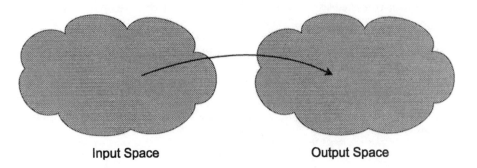

Input Space   Output Space

Figure 13. Abstract Representation of a Complete Solution

By complete solution, it is meant that every possible input from the input space has a corresponding output within the output space. A complete solution is exhaustive. If the function is something simple, like addition, then a solution that can compute integer arithmetic is complete. Given two integers from the input space, the output is computable.

An *incomplete solution* is one that can correctly operate for only a subset of the input space. An example is shown in Figure 14.

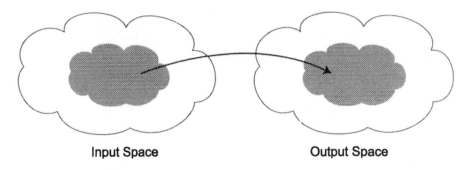

Input Space   Output Space

Figure 14. Abstract Representation of an Incomplete Solution

An important distinction needs to be made between a continuous neural network and the use of the definition of a complete solution. Neural networks that operate upon continuous input and output data can be considered capable of generating an output for any possible permutation of the input variables. But just because they produce an output for all input values, this does not imply the solution is complete. In order to be a complete solution, the neural network would need to be correct (or sufficiently correct from the project's perspective) to qualify as a complete solution.

The implication here is that there is a trade-off between the completeness of the required solution and the capabilities of the computational resources to accommodate the solution. The use of a neural network as a complete or incomplete solution primarily depends upon the available computational resources, and is thus system dependent. An incomplete solution does not contain all possible permutations across the input space. Consequently, the amount of knowledge that a neural network needs to learn becomes smaller and thus easier to obtain.

The definition of the complete solution can be further decomposed:

- *Simple* – A simple complete solution is one that contains a limited number of input-output mappings, perhaps trivial.
- *Complex* – A complex complete solution is one that contains, for practical purposes, an unlimited number of possible input-output pairings, and might be considered computationally challenging.
- *Moderate* – A moderate complete solution falls between the above two categories.

The integer arithmetic solution referred to earlier is complex complete if the input space is unlimited and only defined by all integers. It would be considered simple complete if the input space were limited to the integers 1 through 10. A moderate complete solution would then be anything between the simple complete and the complex complete solutions.

In some ways, an incomplete problem could be considered a simple complete solution for a constrained input space. It really depends upon perspective. If the system input can come from any integer number, and the solution only needs to be correct for a specific subset, it would probably be more appropriate to call it an incomplete solution. If, however, the input space were already constrained, and the solution needed only be correct for the given input space, it would be a simple complete solution.

Because processing power and capabilities are always improving, clear identification of the differences between simple, moderate, and complex may change over time. It is the responsibility of the practitioner to judge the problem domain and decide upon the level of complexity. Use of a neural network for a simple, possibly even a moderately complete problem may be acceptable, but a different solution would be needed for a complex complete problem. A project could be better served through use of multiple neural networks, or a combination of neural networks and other technologies, as opposed to a single neural network solution. A reduction of the complexity within the problem space through conversion to an incomplete problem can simplify the application.

Neural networks are primarily useful for domains in which a total understanding of all possible outcomes is not well known. These problems can be solved by incomplete solutions where only specific input-output mappings are required. Incomplete solutions can also arise because for the problem domain there are input combinations that are impossible to be obtained by a system or because some of the possible input combinations can be ignored as they have little use in solving the problem. Examples of incomplete solutions include classification and pattern recognition in which systems can generalize a solution from a relatively limited number of known target patterns.

Table 4 depicts the abstract concepts of the solution type and identifies the appropriateness of using a neural network for such a solution.

Table 4. Appropriateness of Neural Network Solution by Solution Type

Solution Type	Representation		Appropriateness
	Input Space	Output Space	
Simple Complete			Neural Network Appropriate
Incomplete			Neural Network Appropriate
Moderate Complete			Neural Network Questionable
Complex Complete			Neural Network Inappropriate

2.13.3 Neural Network Systems at a Low Level

When analyzing documentation that identifies the reasons for the neural network selection, the practitioner should be wary of poor rationale and weak arguments. Their occurrences will only strengthen the argument that the project team probably does not know enough about neural networks to be using them correctly in the first place.

Some of the advantages of using neural networks that documentation might cite include:

- Neural networks can be computed in parallel and a parallel architecture is readily available within the target hardware.
- Neural networks can adapt in real time, allowing them to self-organize or structure themselves to a solution.
- Neural networks can derive meaning from complicated data sets (and thus may be

able to provide a partial solution to NP-complete problems).

- Neural networks can overcome noisy data and still generate a correct answer.
- Neural networks are potentially fault tolerant so if a part of the network experiences a fault, the remaining part of the network may still operate correctly. If the network is adaptive, the fault could be compensated for through continued neural network learning.

Failure to explain why the neural network is being used should be considered an immediate red flag. The selection of a neural network solution should be clear and well explained, including presentation within the early project reviews. The following are examples of poor justification and the practitioner should document them as such:

- The team has no experience with neural networks and wishes to broaden their horizons.
- Neural networks are a current trend and the project wants to participate in this trend.
- "Other projects use neural networks."
- "The previous project used neural networks and while we don't know why, we think it was for a good reason."

Of course project documentation will never be as stark as the above examples, but a practitioner should be wary of documentation that essentially means the same thing. Good reasons for using neural networks might resemble:

- The neural network will be able to approximate a function describing the underlying nature of the incoming data, thus allowing the system to compensate for any errors.
- System data will contain varying levels of noise and a neural network solution will be able to compensate for this unpredictable error.
- A neural network classification approach will be faster than the alternatives.
- Project engineers have used neural networks before and feel that the research problem under investigation will do well with a neural network solution. [X] and [Y] serve as a foundation for this reasoning. (Note: [X] and [Y] refer to citations of conference or journal papers, text books, or other authoritative materials.)

In addition to the advantages, the practitioner should be aware of some of the limitations of using a neural network system. Limitations may not be within the project documentation, but addressing the limitations may make the reasoning for their use stronger. Examples of some neural network limitations include:

- When a neural network is used in sequential hardware, it loses the advantages of parallel processing. Computational resources can increase based on the network size, number of inputs, and complexity of learning/growing algorithms. (Also known as the scalability problem.)
- Incorrect or suboptimal preprocessing of the network inputs can affect network success.
- Neural network design is considered more of an art than a science, making some

neural network developers frustrated because they have a difficult time obtaining good solutions.

- Neural networks are not easily verified and there is some distrust of their use in safety- and mission-critical systems.
- Neural networks lack the ability to explain why they behave the way they do.

While it is up to the project to overcome the limitations, there are techniques to reduce them. For instance, rule extraction provides a way to translate the *black box* neural network to a *white box* understanding, thereby eliminating one of the above concerns. The verification and validation of neural networks is the reason for this book, whose intent is to minimize this concern.

2.13.4   Neural Network Taxonomy

Table 5 can be a quick reference as a basic guide for the uses of neural networks. It includes subcategorization and some additional notes about each subcategory of neural network. The table is not absolute as neural network architectures are so versatile and robust that they can often be used for many different applications.

Table 5. Basic Taxonomy of Neural Network Architectures

Base Neural Network Architecture	Example Types	Possible Uses	Notes
Radial Basis	Radial Basis Function	Function approximation	If the complexity of the input space is significant, the radial basis neural networks can be large and computationally expensive. Radial basis neural networks perform well at generalization.
	Generalized Regression Network	Function approximation	
	Probabilistic Neural Network	Classification problems	
Perceptron	Perceptron	Classification problems; function approximation	Perhaps the most common type of neural network in use today. Capable of approximating any continuous-valued function.
	Adaline		
	Multi-Layer Perceptron		
	Back-propagation		
Recurrent	Hopfield	Classification problems; error correction	Recurrent neural networks are a variation of the feed-forward with connections from internal or output layers used as inputs. The Hopfield neural network can learn and store target classifications. Outputs from the Hopfield can only come from these classifications, making it highly robust to poor data integrity.
	Spatio-Temporal Pattern Recognition	Detection/generation of temporal and spatial patterns; signal processing; prediction	
	Boltzmann Machine	Classification problems; error correction	
	Bidirectional Associative Memory	Classification/association problems	
Higher-Order	Sigma-Pi	Non-linear function approximation	Higher-order neural networks are better at non-linear (polynomial) function approximation than feed-forward neural networks.
	Pi-Sigma		
Self-Organizing	Kohonen	Unsupervised clustering; classification; function approximation; topology preservation	Operates through competition between the neurons such that one neuron usually accounts for the output. An output function using neighborhood neurons is also possible.
	Self-Organizing Feature Map		
	Competitive Neural Network		
	Gaseous Cell Structure		
	Dynamic Cell Structure		
Adaptive Resonance	ART-1	Vector classification, data conceptualization	An improperly understood vigilance parameter that controls how much the network adjusts to new patterns could make for sub-optimal performance.
	ART-2		
	Fuzzy ART		

3

VERIFICATION AND VALIDATION OF NEURAL NETWORKS – GUIDANCE

Since this guidance mirrors IEEE Std 1012-1998, the practitioner may benefit from having a copy of that standard available.

IEEE Std 1012 maps easily onto a waterfall development methodology and structures a V&V framework using the terminology of process, activity, and task. Figure 15 illustrates how the V&V processes are subdivided into activities, which in turn have associated tasks.

Although this guidance follows a similar development framework, it too is adjustable based upon a project's needs. For example, the practitioner may want to adjust it for the nested loop model of neural network development discussed in Section 2.5.

Some projects may produce well-defined documentation, strictly adhering to the IEEE Std 1012 recommendations. Other projects may use variations of the IEEE standard's processes, activities, and tasks. The practitioner may refer to the portions of this guidance that address the specific needs of a given project. Projects that produce very detailed documentation at early stages may require the practitioner to apply techniques that are discussed in this guidance related to later stages of the life cycle. A practitioner may always apply guidance from later stages to earlier stages, if the guidance is appropriate.

IEEE Std 1012 defines processes and activities, then lists the associated tasks. This guidance expands upon these tasks and provides key recommendations related to adaptive systems (using neural networks as an example) for six IEEE Std 1012 processes: Management, Acquisition, Supply, Development, Operation, and Maintenance.

This chapter provides information on the task level for which guidance was deemed necessary when applying the IEEE Std 1012 to a system incorporating adaptive software systems, particularly neural networks. Examples and case studies have been included for many of the tasks. Examples are provided as suggestions to further understanding of how to apply the tasks to adaptive software. Case studies are contained in boxes offset to the right of the applicable guidance. The case studies include a small amount of specific details that originate from the IFCS project. The goal of including the case studies is to demonstrate how the task was implemented within a safety- and mission-critical system.

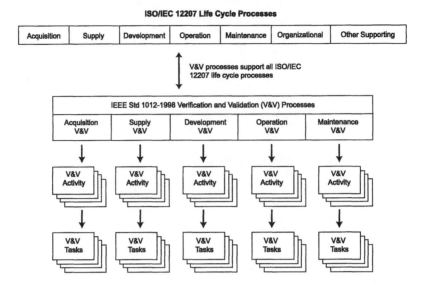

Figure 15. Framework of V&V Processes, Activities, and Tasks

3.1   PROCESS: MANAGEMENT

One activity is found within the overall V&V Management Process, that is, the Management of V&V Activity. This guidance addresses areas within this process where the use of an adaptive system, or specifically the use of a neural network, may require additional attention.

3.1.1   Activity: Management of V&V

The single task found within the V&V Management Process is conducted throughout the entire project life cycle and consists of the five tasks discussed in the following sections.

3.1.1.1   Task: Software Verification and Validation Plan (SVVP) Generation. Required Inputs: SVVP (previous update), Contract, Concept Documentation, Supplier Development Plans and Schedules.

The SVVP identifies the process, activities, and tasks to be completed during a project to ensure high-quality software development. The decision to use an adaptive system will affect the creation of the SVVP. It is therefore recommended that projects making use of adaptive software systems consider all guidance found within this chapter during the creation of the project SVVP.

The SVVP should consider the use of specialized tools to facilitate the certification of the neural network and other adaptive software. Useful tools include neural network development environments, visualization packages, evaluation tools, and test data generators. Specific examples mentioned in this guidance include the NN Evaluator, the Sensitivity Tool, and the Confidence Tool. The project may also develop new tools to use during evaluation. Tools and techniques specifically applicable to neural networks and adaptive systems are discussed in Chapter 2.0. These can be used to supplement the basic activities outlined in the SVVP.

3.1.1.2 Task: Baseline Change Assessment. Required Inputs: SVVP, Proposed Changes, Hazard Analysis Report, Risk Identified by V&V Tasks.

When the project uses adaptive systems, neural networks in particular, the assessment of changes to the software is different than for traditional software. An adaptive system can have two types of changes: traditional software changes and changes in knowledge through adaptation. The project must keep track of these software changes and make sure they comply with requirements.

Changes in knowledge through adaptation are those changes by the neural network occurring during typical operations. These must be tracked to ensure compliance with requirements. Neural network adaptations may occur frequently because of training, architectural modification, input/output modifications, or learning and growing algorithm refinement. These changes relate to knowledge acquisition and storage, the impact of which can be just as significant as changing the functionality of a software module. In fact, changes to the knowledge acquisition and encapsulation should be treated exactly as a change in functionality because the new neural network will perform a different approximation function than it did before the change.

When these changes occur during the design phase of the life cycle, tracking them can be burdensome and daunting. To alleviate this burden and still meet the necessary traceability needs, baseline change assessment may be postponed while the neural network is undergoing many modifications as the developers try to achieve system requirements. After the neural network design has reached some level of maturity, likely during the implementation or testing stages, then baseline change assessment should be considered.

The premise behind baseline change assessment is to give the V&V practitioner (and the developer) confidence that the impacts due to modification of the software are identified, evaluated, and deemed acceptable. This should also be the premise behind judging the appropriateness of changes made to the neural network.

The following list includes areas for consideration when identifying and evaluating change:

- ensuring the training sets used during additional neural network adaptation are identified, including the order in which the training sets are applied, the number of training iterations, outputs of the network during training, and the neural network error functions;
- identifying a clear description of the intended changes to the neural network, the changes made to the training set, the expected change in the neural network outputs; and
- identifying the impact to schedule and cost from applying changes to the neural network.

Reasons a neural network might require change are:

- The network exhibits too high an error during component-level testing or integration testing.
- The operating environment changes or becomes better defined.

- New training data has been collected during the life of the project. The new data may suggest that previous data is no longer current, no longer accurate, or is otherwise incomplete.
- Another component in the system changes due to test results or other modification. This can happen especially when the neural network's design and operation are closely tied to another component in the system. When the neural network has been refined for a specific knowledge and the system changes, the knowledge acquisition or knowledge encapsulation may need to be updated or changed.

Possible adverse effects the practitioner should guard against include:

- The addition of newer knowledge into the neural network may reduce the accuracy of the neural network, overgeneralize the neural network, or corrupt the existing knowledge.
- Due to excessive changing of training sets or modifications within the system, the neural network development never seems completed and begins to impact project schedules and cost.

3.1.1.3   Task: Management Review of V&V. Required Inputs: SVVP and Updates, Supplier Development Plans and Schedules, V&V task results.

Analyzing and reviewing the V&V process is equally as important for a system that contains an adaptive element as it is for a system that does not contain an adaptive element. However, project managers and other management personnel may have special concerns about V&V of adaptive software, especially when this software could affect the safety of humans or the environment. Therefore, it may be necessary to provide a management overview of the special neural network considerations discussed in Chapter 2.0.

3.1.1.4   Task: Management and Technical Review Support. Required Inputs: V&V task results, Materials for review [e.g., software requirements specification (SRS), interface requirements specification (IRS), software design description (SDD), interface design document (IDD), test documents].

For this task, the practitioner will want to ensure that personnel with appropriate adaptive system development background and experience attend reviews and meetings. When discussing highly critical components of the system that contain adaptive elements, the practitioner will want to ensure that the review process is thorough and not rushed, to encourage participation from those attending the review. Reviews can make use of visual depictions, neural network rule extraction, and demonstrations to ensure that all in attendance gain a general understanding of the neural network system.

**Case Study Example 1.
Neural Network
Visualizations for Reviews**

Early in the development of IFCS GEN1, the DCS neural network structure was plotted across time. These plots were assembled and presented as a video during an early project meeting. From this video, the project team gained a basic understanding of how the DCS learns and grows.

3.1.1.5   Task: Interface With Organizational and Support Processes. Required Inputs: SVVP, Data identified in the SVVP for organizational and supporting processes.

No guidance has been developed for this task. The coordination between organizational and support processes does not change and the V&V data that needs to be exchanged between these processes will not necessarily change due to the inclusion of adaptive elements within the system.

3.2   PROCESS: ACQUISITION

During the Acquisition Process, the V&V team scopes the V&V effort, plans interfaces with the supplier and acquirer, and reviews the draft systems requirements contained in the request for proposal (RFP). Before Acquisition, the SVVP is established and so any tasks related to the use of adaptive or neural network systems should have already been included in the SVVP. However, based upon the system, tailoring of the SVVP can occur. Impacts to the project schedule, budget, and top-level system requirements can result based on the practitioner recommendations.

3.2.1   Activity: Acquisition Support V&V

Three tasks fall within the Acquisition Support V&V Activity. For each of these, the following sections identify considerations for the practitioner when the project plans to use an adaptive or neural network system.

3.2.1.1 Task: Scoping the V&V Effort. Required Inputs: Preliminary System Description, Statement of Need (RFP), System Integrity Level Scheme.

The Scoping of the V&V Effort Task provides for the establishment and assignment of software integrity levels (Table 6), as well as what V&V processes, activities, and tasks are required. The practitioner can tailor the IEEE Std 1012 tasks to be performed based upon system criticality. The practitioner should also consider the augmentation of V&V activities presented in this book addressed specifically to adaptive or neural network systems.

**Case Study Example 2.
Adaptive System Criticality**

The IFCS adaptive systems were assigned software criticality using IEEE 1012-1998 integrity levels as well a NASA Dryden classification scheme for flight software. Based on this scheme, the criticality of the adaptive system was reduced due to the dependence upon external safety monitors.

Table 6. Software Integrity Levels in IEEE Std 1012-1998 [IEEE 1998]

Criticality	Description	Level
High	Selected function affects critical performance of the system.	4
Major	Selected function affects important system performance.	3
Moderate	Selected function affects system performance, but workaround strategies can be implemented to compensate for loss of performance.	2
Low	Selected function has noticeable effect on system performance but only creates inconvenience to the user if the function does not perform in accordance with requirements.	1

This guidance is based upon the IEEE Std 1012-1998; it is recommended that the practitioner study both the IEEE standard and this guidance to identify appropriate augmentation to the V&V processes.

3.2.1.2 *Task: Planning the Interface between the V&V Effort and Supplier.* Required Inputs: SVVP, RFP, Contract, Supplier Development Plans and Schedules.

During this task, the supplier's development plans and schedules are used to identify how the V&V process can be incorporated into the schedule. Here it is critical to consider the level of experience and expertise of the team conducting the review of adaptive systems. A lack of experience with adaptive or neural network systems will likely increase the difficulty in performing concept V&V and design V&V and thus the time it takes to complete these processes. Certainly other V&V processes, including the Requirements and Testing Processes, will also be affected by the level of experience the supplier's team has with adaptive systems. However, the highest impact will probably come during the initial concept stages of the project and then the subsequent training/design of the adaptive or neural network components.

The most important thing to consider is when in doubt, include additional time for the V&V of adaptive systems. This time may be required to thoroughly analyze the development, to become familiar with development tools, to develop new analysis techniques and tools, and to gain a better understanding of the type of adaptive system.

3.2.1.3 *Task: System Requirements Review.* Required Inputs: Preliminary System Description, Statement of Need, User Needs, RFP.

System Requirements Review involves evaluation of top-level system requirements for two purposes. The first is to validate whether the requirements can be satisfied by the defined technologies, methods, and algorithms defined for the project (feasibility), and verify whether objective information that can be demonstrated by testing is provided in the requirements (testability). In order to evaluate if any specifications requiring the use of an adaptive system can meet the overall system requirements, the practitioner must evaluate whether a general adaptive system or a neural network is appropriate. Much of this discussion is found in Section 2.13.

The second purpose is to verify the consistency of requirement to user needs. Requirements related to adaptive behavior are difficult to write and should address two aspects:

- how the adaptive system acquires knowledge and acts on that knowledge (Control), and
- what knowledge the adaptive system should acquire (Knowledge).

To verify consistency of the requirements to the user needs, first the user needs related to the adaptive system must be clearly defined. These needs should be documented in early project documents or the RFP. Documents at this stage should contain high-level goals for the adaptive system. These high-level goals should first be stated in early documents and then be traceable through systems requirements and software requirements. To make traceability easier throughout the process, these goals should be summarized in a table at the end of the document.

Table 7 gives an example of high-level goals (HLGs) for an online adaptive neural network used in an intelligent-flight-control application.

Table 7. Example High-Level Goals for an Online Adaptive Neural Network

Identifier	High-Level Goal
HLG 1.1.2	Information from the neural networks shall help optimize aircraft performance in both normal and failure conditions.
HLG 1.3.1	The online adaptive neural network shall learn changes in the baseline F-15 test aircraft stability and control derivatives and upgrade the neural network representations.
HLG 1.4.1	The adaptive flight controller shall adjust flight control performance to maintain consistent aircraft dynamics during simulated failures.
HLG 2.2.1	The online adaptive neural network shall sense the simulated failures and adjust the control strategy to provide the best possible flying qualities.
HLG 6.1.1	The online adaptive neural network shall learn and store aircraft stability and control derivatives that will be used to automatically adjust control law gains for desirable aircraft dynamics.

3.3   PROCESS: SUPPLY

The Supply Process V&V involves tying the SVVP into the developer schedule and making sure all parties on the project have established a means of communication that will enable V&V. This also applies to adaptive or neural network systems.

3.3.1   Activity: Planning V&V

Two items are suggested for the practitioner during the planning V&V activity:

- Special consideration should be given to the impact on the schedule and cost associated with V&V of adaptive or neural network systems, which is heavily influenced by the level of experience of the V&V team.
- For rare cases in which the adaptive system can create original information or solutions, ownership of this new material needs to be clearly identified.

3.3.1.1 Task: Planning the Interface between the V&V Effort and Supplier. Required Inputs: SVVP, Supplier Development Plans and Schedules.

As this task is almost the same as the Acquisition V&V Task of interface planning between the V&V effort and supplier, the same advice applies. Based upon the level of experience and comfort in working with an adaptive or neural network system, the practitioner may want to ensure the schedule adequately reflects any schedule risk by providing adequate time to conduct V&V tasking.

3.3.1.2 Task: Contract Verification. Required Inputs: SVVP, RFP, Contract, User Needs, Supplier Development Plans and Schedules.

Careful consideration of intellectual property rights for the adaptive system may be necessary. A unique situation could arise when defining ownership of, or intellectual property rights for, an adaptive system. Research is constantly pushing the capabilities of artificial intelligence and it is conceivable that an adaptive system itself will one day be able to create new intellectual property. If this is possible for the current project, this concern should be addressed. Keep this in mind when verifying contract documents. For example, consider a situation in which an adaptive system is a centralized brain that creates new plans or can generate software to solve problems in real time. The practitioner may want to ensure that any new plans or software modules have a clear designation of ownership.

3.4   PROCESS: DEVELOPMENT

The Development Process section contains the majority of the guidance related to adaptive/ neural network systems. By this time in the life cycle the developer should have decided on the specific technology to implement the adaptive components of the system. Much of the guidance beyond the Concept V&V Activity will be specific to neural networks.

3.4.1   Activity: Concept V&V

Within the Concept V&V Activity, the IEEE Std 1012 identifies six different tasks. These tasks are addressed in the following sections.

3.4.1.1 Task: Concept Documentation Evaluation. Required Inputs: Concept Documentation, Supplier Development Plans and Schedules, User Needs, Acquisition Needs.

The purpose of Concept Documentation Evaluation is to analyze the concept documents to determine if they meet the user or project needs and are consistent with documentation from previous activities. Documents created during the Concept V&V Activity may include Statement of Need, Advance Planning Report, Project Initialization Memo, Project Plan, Objectives and Requirements, Feasibility Studies, and Systems Requirements.

At this stage in the life cycle, the practitioner may be faced with concept documentation that falls into one of the following categories:

- *Category 1*: No reference is made to an adaptive system,
- *Category 2*: A reference is made to an adaptive system but no specific technology for implementation is named, or
- *Category 3*: A specific reference is made to adaptive neural networks.

The recommended guidance varies based upon the category.

Category 1: No Adaptive Software System. No guidance is required for this category because the practitioner is only dealing with traditional software development.

Category 2: Reference Made to an Adaptive Software System. When the project does not reference a specific adaptive software technology, the practitioner should check that the following is true of the concept documentation:

- Make sure that Concept Documentation talks about the adaptive nature of the system.
- Make sure the adaptive nature of the system is captured in the requirements.
- If migrating from a nonadaptive system to an adaptive system, make sure the adaptive system specification is complete.

The documents at this stage should contain high-level goals for the adaptive system and system requirements that cover both control and knowledge.

Category 3: Reference Made to an Adaptive Neural Network. When the project makes a reference to the use of neural networks, or even a specific type of neural network, the practitioner should check many of the items from category 2 in addition to looking for information related to the neural network.

- As with category 2, make sure that Concept Documentation talks about the adaptive nature of the neural network and that the adaptive nature of the neural network is described somewhere. Items that a practitioner may want to verify exist include constraints on the computational resources used by the neural network, what specifically the neural network will learn, when the neural network is to learn, and so on.
- Verify that the rationale for using the neural network is documented.
- If a specific neural network is chosen, make sure that rationale is provided for why this neural network will be used.

The documents at this stage should contain high-level goals and system requirements that flow down to the neural network. Table 8 gives an example of high-level goals for an online adaptive neural network used in an intelligent flight control application mapped to the system requirements.

The system requirements should also address the two aspects already referred to in Section 3.2.1.3. These aspects are

- *Control* – how the adaptive system acquires knowledge and acts on that knowledge, and
- *Knowledge* – what knowledge the adaptive system should acquire.

Table 9 shows examples of system-level requirements related to neural network control.

Table 10 shows examples of system-level requirements related to neural network knowledge.

Table 8. Example High-Level Goals and System Requirements for an Online Adaptive Neural Network

High-level Goals	System Requirements
HLG 1.1.2. Information from the neural networks shall help optimize aircraft performance in both normal and failure conditions.	3.2.4.4-01. A pilot-selectable switch shall be provided to engage and disengage simulated failure modes. 3.10.3.1-03. The neural net software shall be used with an adaptive flight controller, which will optimize aircraft performance to maintain desirable handling qualities during both normal flight conditions and simulated flight control failures.
HLG 1.3.1. The on-line neural network (OLNN) shall learn changes in the baseline F-15 test aircraft stability and control derivatives and upgrade the neural network representations.	3.2.4.1-11. A pilot-selectable switch shall be provided to allow the OLNN algorithm to be reset during flight.
HLG 1.4.1. The adaptive flight controller shall adjust flight control performance to maintain consistent aircraft dynamics during simulated failures.	3.10.3.1-02. The IFCS neural net software shall be able to learn and store aircraft stability and control derivatives errors that will in turn be used to adjust the control law gains for the desirable aircraft dynamics.
HLG 2.2.1. The OLNN shall sense the simulated failures and adjust the control strategy to provide the best possible flying qualities.	3.10.3.3-02. The online learning neural network software shall interpret results from the PTNN and the real-time parameter identification algorithm and output corrections to the baseline stability and control derivatives for the aircraft during flight.
HLG 6.1.1. The OLNN shall learn and store aircraft stability and control derivatives that will be used to automatically adjust control law gains for desirable aircraft dynamics.	3.10.3.1-02. The IFCS neural net software shall be able to learn and store aircraft stability and control derivatives errors that will in turn be used to adjust the control law gains for the desirable aircraft dynamics.

Table 9. Example System Requirements for Neural Networks Related to Control

System Requirement Identifier	System Requirement Description
3.2.4.1-04	The derivative corrections for the online learning neural network algorithm shall be output for the post-test analysis.
3.3.5-05	The corrected stability and control derivatives output from the online learning neural network software shall be output to the instrumentation system via the ARTS II Experiment multiplexer (MUX).
3.10.3.1-01	The ARTS II computer shall utilize a real-time operating system and host the pre-trained neural network, online learning neural network, and parameter identification software.
3.10.4-02	The ARTS II shall support the processing of the online learning neural networks at a minimum frame of 40 Hz.

Table 10. Example System Requirements for Neural Networks Related to Knowledge

System Requirement Identifier	System Requirement Description
3.10.3.1-02	The IFCS neural net software shall be able to learn and store aircraft stability and control derivatives errors that will in turn be used to adjust the control law gains for the desirable aircraft dynamics.
3.10.3.1-03	The neural net software shall be used with an adaptive flight controller, which will optimize aircraft performance to maintain desirable handling qualities during both normal flight conditions and simulated flight control failures.
3.10.3.3-02	The online learning neural network software shall interpret results from the PTNN and the real-time parameter identification algorithm and output corrections to the baseline stability and control derivatives for the aircraft during flight.

3.4.1.2 Task: Criticality Analysis. Required Inputs: Concept Documentation (System Requirements), developer integrity level assignments.

The Criticality Analysis Task ensures that a project has established criteria for designating software integrity levels and that these levels have been assigned appropriately to some segmentation of the software being developed.

Considering only the directives provided in IEEE Std 1012, there is no recommended additional guidance for systems that make use of adaptive systems, or neural networks. The criticality of a component at the concept stage (in which system functionality is allocated to Computer Software Component (CSC) or module level) is not based on its implementation but on its function. Whether the module functionality is implemented via a neural network or traditional software, a failure of the module would have the same impact. Neural networks do not affect criticality at the concept stage.

Case Study Example 3. IFCS CSC Criticality

The adaptive systems developed for the IFCS project were placed in a self-contained research computer. Criticality was assigned to each CSC in the computer. These included:
- *Ground Support Software,*
- *Operational Monitors, and*
- *Direct Adaptive Neural Network.*

3.4.1.3 Task: Hardware/Software/User Requirements Allocation Analysis. Required Inputs: User Needs, Concept Documentation.

For correctness considerations, the practitioner will want to verify that any requirements levied against the adaptive system include at least a high-level description of acceptable behavior. Examples of behaviors for the adaptive system can include stability, timing constraints for adaptation, production of outputs, or defined regions of operation. Defining the region of operation is crucial because the size of the region can affect the adaptive system computational resource needs, the system's accuracy, internal knowledge representation, and design of the knowledge acquisition functions.

For completeness considerations, the practitioner will want to verify that ideas are expressed within the concept documentation facilitating online adaptive system error detection and recovery. Because online adaptive systems will continue to change during operation, having a means to detect improper learning and preventing this from affecting system safety and mission success is required. Detailed solutions may not be needed within the concept documentation, but the documents should be written to enable the software requirements to be derived.

3.4.1.4 Task: Traceability Analysis. Required Inputs: Concept Documentation.

During this task, the V&V effort identifies all system requirements that will be implemented fully or partially by software. Refer to Concept Documentation Evaluation, Section 3.4.1.1, for a discussion of high-level goals traced to systems requirements. The high-level goals that pertain to the adaptive nature of the system can assist in tracing the system requirements to the acquisition needs. Tracing between system requirements and software requirements that pertain to the knowledge can be assisted through the use of rule extraction techniques. Refer to Sections 2.3 and 2.4, respectively, for discussions of knowledge requirements and rule extraction.

3.4.1.5 Task: Hazard Analysis. Required Inputs: Concept Documentation.

A preliminary hazard analysis can be conducted by use of HAZOPs. Assuming that the system is only discussed as an adaptive system (meaning no specific type of adaptation, such as a neural network system, has been specified), then the following potential hazards of an adaptive system should be considered for the HAZOPs:

> **Case Study Example 4.**
> **IFCS GEN2 Requirements**
> **Allocation Analysis**
>
> IFCS GEN2 system requirements were verified through allocation analysis. Below are examples of correctness and completeness checks.
>
> The requirement: *The IFCS GEN2 system shall use an online learning neural network to adjust the feedback errors to achieve desired system behavior in the presence of off nominal behavior or failures.* Contributes to correctness because it discusses performance and links to high-level goals.
>
> The requirement: *A safety monitor shall be developed to disengage the research mode when OLNN stability and control derivative corrections exceed a predetermined safe range.* Contributes to completeness because it proposes neural network error detection and recovery, which touches upon functionality, fault detection, and error recovery.

- The system does not adapt.
- The system adapts, but is unable to reach convergence (adaptive system is divergent, adaptive system undergoes oscillation).
- The system adapts and converges, but converges to an incorrect state (incorrect error compensation, incorrect classification).
- The network grows beyond available system resources during adaptation (lack of boundaries on the growth, lack of acceptable growing limits).
- The system converges to a correct state, but cannot do so in the required time (timeliness issues).

Another approach to hazard analysis is the use of Preliminary Hazard Identifications (PHI) and Functional Hazard Analysis (FHA) from Kurd [Kurd 2003], mentioned in Section 2.5.2, Safety Life Cycle for Hybrid Neural Networks (see Figure 9). A development life cycle for "hybrid" neural networks is based upon three main levels: symbolic, translation, and neural learning. PHI addresses initial symbolic knowledge and is used to determine the initial conditions of the network. PHI attempts to understand potential hazards in real-world terms. The identification of potential hazards and generation of system level hazards (using a black-box approach) may result in a set of rules partially fulfilling the desired function. Knowledge should be gathered from domain experts, empirical data, and other sources.

The PHI is followed by an FHA performed over the subinitial symbolic knowledge through a predictive, systematic, white-box style technique. The purpose of the FHA is to understand how the symbolic knowledge can lead to hazards. FHA develops an understanding of certain rules, can facilitate "targeted" training, and may make rule assertions to prevent specific hazards. Both the subinitial symbolic information from the PHI and initial symbolic information from the FHA may be described as rules to be used within the requirements generation process.

3.4.1.6 Task: Risk Analysis. Required Inputs: Concept Documentation, Supplier Development Plans and Schedules, Hazard Analysis Report, V&V task results.

The Risk Analysis Task must consider risks from both a management and a technical perspective. In terms of assessing management risk, the practitioner will want to determine if the project and project team have sufficient knowledge to develop adaptive systems, depending on how specified the project is by the concept stage. For example, if the project documentation discusses neural networks, a prudent observation would be to determine if the corresponding team members have expertise in designing, implementing, testing, and analyzing neural networks. From the technical risk standpoint, the analysis needs to concentrate on the justification for the use of an adaptive solution.

**Case Study Example 5.
IFCS GEN2 Preliminary
OLNN Hazards**

The preliminary hazard analysis of IFCS GEN2 identified several hazards associated with neural networks. The following are a few of the hazards from this analysis:

- *The OLNN fails to adapt.*
- *The OLNN adapts incorrectly.*
- *The OLNN does not adapt within timing requirements.*
- *The OLNN produces non-zero feedback when in the OFF state.*
- *The OLNN continues to adapt while in the OFF state.*
- *The OLNN cannot change gain sets for flight testing.*
- *The OLNN cannot change learning rates for a flight test.*
- *The OLNN cannot change adaptation gains for a flight test.*
- *The OLNN weights are initialized incorrectly.*

Each hazard was evaluated for frequency of occurrence and severity of failure to plan for sufficient mitigation. Use of a safety monitor was cited as the mitigation strategy for the hazards listed above.

**Case Study Example 6.
IFCS GEN2 Preliminary
OLNN Risks**

Some risks were identified in IFCS GEN2 as a result of planning to use a neural network. They included:
- *Lack of Sigma-Pi mathematical foundation, and*
- *Lack of Sigma-Pi testing techniques.*

3.4.2   Activity: Requirements V&V

For this guidance, it is assumed that during the Requirements V&V Activity of the project, the discussion of the use of adaptive systems within the project evolves into the more specific reference to neural networks. By the Requirements V&V Activity, a project that plans to utilize a neural network should, at a minimum, include discussion of neural networks within the software requirements documentation. If a neural network is to be employed, it is likely that the project has already made reference to neural networks earlier in the documentation and, thus, the practitioner can use this guidance at whatever stage in the project it is useful.

Software requirements related to adaptive behavior are difficult to write. Specifically for neural networks, the software requirements (just as the system requirements) must address the two aspects mentioned earlier for high-level goals and system requirements:

- *Control* – how the adaptive system acquires knowledge and acts on that knowledge, and
- *Knowledge* – what knowledge the adaptive system should acquire.

Functional requirements related to the *control* of the neural network are easier to write and are the same as those found in typical software requirements documentation. These requirements should address areas such as:

- algorithmic capabilities,
- hardware specifications,
- operating capabilities,
- input/output,
- data recording capabilities,
- training inputs, and
- stopping criteria.

Table 11 provides an example of software requirements related to control written for an adaptive neural network in an intelligent flight control system.

Table 11. Example Neural Network Software Requirements Related to Control

Software Requirement
The online neural network shall accept the following 12 sensor inputs: mach, altitude, left stabilator deflection, right stabilator deflection, left rudder deflection, right rudder deflection, left aileron deflection, right aileron deflection, left canard deflection, and right canard deflection.
The online neural network shall compute 26 stability and control derivatives.
The online neural network module shall utilize less than 500K of memory.
The online neural network shall retain prior learning experience or reset back to an *a priori* state as the ARTS II (Airborne Research Test System, 2nd Generation) Computer Software Configuration Item (CSCI) transitions between ENGAGED or DISENGAGED states.

Functional requirements related to the *knowledge* of the neural network may be more difficult to define. Neural network requirements related to knowledge:

- should address the knowledge that will be gained by the adaptive system during training and operation,
- will be necessarily incomplete at the beginning of the Development Process. (This incompleteness is caused by insufficient data or expert domain knowledge to develop the complete solution, which led to the use of an adaptive system in the beginning.), and
- will not represent the entire target function or solution.

Table 12 gives an example of software requirements related to knowledge written for an adaptive neural network in an intelligent flight control system.

Table 12. Example Neural Network Software Requirements Related to Knowledge

Software Requirement
The pretrained neural network shall have maximum error of 15% training error from wind-tunnel-table training data.
The pretrained neural network shall have Root Mean Square errors less than 5% from the wind-tunnel-table training data.
The online neural network shall have maximum error of 15% training error from wind-tunnel-table training data.
The online neural network software shall be able to learn and store aircraft stability and control derivatives errors that, in turn, will be used to adjust the control law gains for the desirable aircraft dynamics.
The neural network shall be used with the flight controller, which will optimize aircraft performance to maintain desirable handling during both normal flight conditions and simulated control failures.

3.4.2.1 Task: Traceability Analysis. Required Inputs: Concept Documentation (System Requirements), SRS, IRS.

Traceability Analysis verifies the traceability down from the systems requirements (concept documents) to the software requirements (SRS and IRS) as well as up from the software requirements to the system level requirements. Analysis should identify relationships for correctness, consistency, completeness, and accuracy.

Techniques, such as rule insertion/extraction, outlined in Section 2.4, that apply specifically to neural networks can help address completeness, making sure that the software requirements related to the neural network knowledge have a sufficient level of detail so they can be traced throughout the life cycle documentation.

3.4.2.2 Task: Software Requirements Evaluation. Required Inputs: Concept Documentation, SRS, IRS.

Software Requirements Evaluation examines the requirements of the SRS and IRS related to the six areas of correctness, consistency, completeness, accuracy, readability, and testability.

Within the Software Requirements Evaluation Task, this guidance focusses on addressing the qualities of completeness and readability. Completeness also requires the addition of two new directives to supplement the IEEE Std 1012.

Evaluating Completeness of Neural Network Software Requirements. The assessment of completeness for software requirements of traditional systems seeks to ensure that requirements have included appropriate functionality, interface descriptions, performance and evaluation criteria, and software control features. When neural networks are specified within the requirements, the practitioner needs to consider these same attributes; however, there are additional top-level directives that need to be added. IEEE Std 1012 [IEEE 1998] Software Requirements Evaluation task directives include:

- Verify that the following elements are in the SRS and IRS, within the assumptions and constraints of the system: functionality; process definitions and scheduling; hardware, software, and user interface descriptions; performance criteria; critical configuration data; and system, device, and software control.
- Verify that the SRS and IRS satisfy specified configuration management procedures.

In addition to these directives, it is suggested that for adaptive systems, and specifically neural network systems, practitioners consider additional directives that are not included in IEEE Std 1012. These new directives have been written to fit with the style of the IEEE standard and are broken into both control and knowledge considerations. The first two directives below are intended for general adaptive software systems, while the latter two are intended for neural network systems. It is entirely reasonable that a practitioner may want to use both sets of new directives or subsets of both during their evaluation. This can be dependent upon the level of detail found within the requirements documentation and the practitioner's potential need to be flexible.

Case Study Example 7. IFCS GEN1 Neural Network Software Requirements with Suggested Areas for Evaluating Completeness

Software Requirement	Suggested Area
The PTNN shall be a fixed, non-adaptive neural network.	Architecture
The PTNN shall have Root Mean Square errors less than 5% from wind-tunnel-training data.	Evaluation metrics
While in the LEARNING mode, the OLNN shall produce a predicted result based upon the sensor data from the current time slice.	Performance
The OLNN shall be in LEARNING mode for only those derivatives whose estimates are considered valid by a confidence measure.	Learning control

For adaptive systems, verify the following control elements are in the SRS or IRS, within the assumptions and constraints of the system (additional directive 1):

- *Convergence* – Proving that the adaptive system can converge within a specified amount of time is a necessity to allow use of the adaptive system within safety- and mission-critical systems. The project should provide specifications describing time of convergence, metrics to evaluate convergence, and perhaps identification of divergence.

- *Growth* – As with traditional software, the neural network requirements should discuss control requirements. This includes specifying when the neural network will be allowed to grow (utilize additional computational resources over time) and to what size/ limit the adaptive structure is allowed to adapt.
- *Performance* – High-level requirements can be written to describe the neural network performance such as output rate frequency, input rate frequency, and other algorithm timing constraints such as convergence times.
- *Learning* – The project should consider controls on the learning of the adaptive system. Where growth is concerned about the size to which the adaptive system can expand, learning is more concerned with when it is appropriate to adapt. Possible specifications for learning include descriptions of when the system is allowed to adapt, when the system is not allowed to adapt, the duration for adaptation to an input stimulus, and evaluation methods.
- *Operational Monitoring* – When a project team believes the adaptive

**Case Study Example 8.
IFCS GEN2 Neural Network Software
Requirements with Suggested Areas for
Evaluating Completeness**

Software Requirement	Suggested Area
The research computer shall execute Sigma-Pi as defined by the Sigma-Pi Design report.	Architecture
The research computer shall initialize the Sigma-Pi tunable parameters based on the contents of the configurable parameter set.	Initialization
Due to the limitations of the MIL-STD-1553B bus, the outputs of the Sigma-Pi shall undergo scaling to shift the values for output to the reference model.	Input
The learning rate for each axis of the OLNN shall be configurable by means of parameter sets.	Learning
In LEARNING mode, the OLNN axes which are ON shall generate augmented commands at a rate of 80 Hz.	Performance
The OLNN Evaluator shall analyze the OLNN weights and error terms to compute norms that will indicate any anomalies in the OLNN.	Operational monitor

system presents too high of a technical risk to be used within a safety- or mission-critical sub-system, the project will want to specify the use of operational monitors. Operational monitors are discussed in Section 2.6.

For adaptive systems, verify the following knowledge elements are in the SRS or IRS, within the assumptions and constraints of the system (additional directive 2):

- *Knowledge Initialization* – In some cases, the project may need to develop requirements that describe the procedures for initializing the adaptive system. Concerns with initialization can include how the adaptive system will initialize and to what values the system will initialize.
- *Knowledge Limits* – Some knowledge requirements may need to set limits for the system or define undesirable behaviors that are not permitted. The later type of requirement can be stated in the negative. For example: "The system shall NOT

(do specific undesirable behavior)." Knowledge requirements that restrict the system from engaging in unacceptable behavior may be easier to formulate and test than requirements that capture the innumerable possibilities for acceptable behavior. Since the knowledge changes during operation, it could be checked continuously or periodically during operation to see if it continues to meet the requirements of the system. A promising technique to achieve this is to create an operational monitor that checks neural network behavior and output against the knowledge requirements, for example, in the form of rules or boundary conditions. The knowledge requirements should be testable. The testing can be assisted by various techniques, including rule extraction and automated test generation.

For neural network systems, verify that the following control elements are in the SRS or IRS (additional directive 3):

- *Architecture Type* – Different neural networks are applied to different problem domains. While no complete taxonomy exists that identifies appropriate neural network architecture selection, there are general guidelines. Some of these can be found in Chapter 4 of [Taylor 2005] and in Section 2.13.4.
- *Input/Output* – Input and output requirements for neural networks are very important. Since neural networks may work upon many different inputs, one concern is that the inputs be scaled such that a large magnitude of one of the inputs does not mask any effect from the other inputs. This introduces scaling issues. The outputs of the neural network may need to be recorded for later offline analysis. The practitioner will want to verify that data recording requirements are complete.
- *Learning Algorithm* – Determine whether the neural network knowledge accumulates over time or is discarded periodically.
- *Evaluation Metrics* – For adaptive neural networks, evaluation criteria for the neural network(s) should be specified. Evaluation criteria can include error metrics, adaptation time, and a measure of internal weight changes. These evaluation metrics can be used internally by the neural network system to adjust operation, or externally by a system judging the confidence of the neural network operation.
- *Neural Network Hardware Specifications* – Some neural networks may require specific hardware requirements. These can include special processors and/or special memory needs.

For neural network systems, verify that the following knowledge elements are in the SRS or IRS (additional directive 4):

- *Neural Network Initialization* – Software requirements may be needed to describe the process of initializing the neural network knowledge. For example, will the knowledge be loaded from a data file, given to the neural network by another software module or system, or will it be different for each initialization. For online adaptive neural networks, initialization may be consistent each time, always set to zero representing no initial knowledge, or it may be a randomization of the network weights. Software requirements may also be needed to identify when or what events within the system will cause initializations to occur.

- *Neural Network Training* – If the neural networks are to be fixed, or are to have a basic set of information prior to their deployment, the project should specify the training set data that will be used for training. These requirements include the type of training data that the neural network training should use, the source of the training data, and the expected level of accuracy between the neural network and the training data.

The practitioner should identify the existence of requirements that address these areas of concern, and then assess these requirements for completeness.

Evaluating Readability of Neural Network Software Requirements. The evaluation of software requirements readability should ensure that the SRS and IRS documentation is legible, understandable, and unambiguous. The neural network is based on statistics and mathematics, and, thus, the requirements should be written to describe the intended knowledge for the software and may need to be in mathematical, formal notation.

One approach to developing the functional requirement(s) related to the neural network knowledge is to model, or describe the knowledge to be acquired, in the form of rules. Experts or those involved in development can translate knowledge requirements into symbolic rules called *subinitial knowledge.*

To facilitate a sufficient level of detail in the different requirements associated with the neural network, a process to use rule extraction to develop system knowledge is described below and illustrated in Figure 16. This process can assist in the traceability between the various levels of requirements and symbolic knowledge.

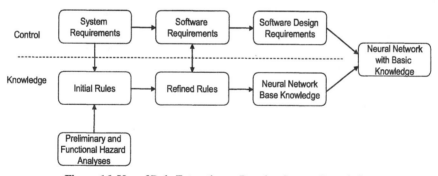

Figure 16. Use of Rule Extraction to Develop System Knowledge

Step 1: Translate System Specifications dealing with the function, basic knowledge, and constraints of the neural network into initial symbolic information in the form of a rule base for the system. These rules can also include information from the Preliminary and Functional Hazard Analyses to address what the neural network is not allowed to do or learn. These initial rules should be translated into a format that can be inserted into the neural network (architecture specific).

Step 2: Refine initial rules and translate them into software requirements. The process of refining the rules may include prototyping the neural network, inserting the initial symbolic knowledge, training the neural network to allow the rules to adapt to the training sets, and extracting the rules.

Step 3: Translate refined rules into a format (neural network architecture specific) that can be inserted into the neural network.

3.4.2.3 Task: Interface Analysis. Required Inputs: Concept Documentation (System Requirements), SRS, IRS.

Interface Analysis verifies that the interfaces described within the system requirements and the SRS and IRS are correct, consistent, complete, accurate, and testable. This guidance recommends that the practitioner give special consideration to the qualities of completeness and accuracy when a project is using neural networks.

Neural networks operate by statistical approaches to data understanding. Because of this, they are susceptible to statistical skewing by differences within the input data. For example, if two inputs are used by the neural network to learn a pattern, and one of these signals is on the order of 100 times greater than the other, the network will tend to give more significance to the higher-magnitude signal. In essence, the larger signal can drown out the smaller signal.

One way to design the neural network to eliminate this effect is to properly scale the input signals. Scaling acts like a normalization by which input values are adjusted to fit within a smaller range while the neural network is still able to learn information about the inputs.

Other preprocessing techniques may also need to be considered based upon the characteristics of the data. These include techniques that:

- smooth the input data to reduce the effects of noise,
- interpolate input data that may have different sampling rates,
- extrapolate the input data due to missing data or to merge different data sets into one, and
- down-sample input data to reduce the data set size to obtain more meaningful data features.

Case Study Example 9. Neural Network Input Scaling

The IFCS GEN1 and GEN2 adaptive systems made use of pre-processing functions to scale inputs to the neural networks. These functions used sets of predetermined values that were loaded from a configuration file upon initialization of the neural networks.

Input preprocessing can be applied to fixed or adaptive neural networks. During the training of a neural network that will later be fixed, the preprocessing can be done on training and testing data that is known in advance. Down-sampling and extrapolation can be used when data, that has been collected from different sources is being used.

During adaptation for an online adaptive neural network, the preprocessing can be designed based upon the developer's best understanding of the expected input signal values. Another alternative, although one that needs close scrutiny for correctness, is that the preprocessing can itself change while online. A system may have little knowledge of the type of noise to expect, and in some situations the noise can reduce the signal-to-noise ratio so much that inputs into the neural network will degrade beyond usefulness. Adaptive filters may be a way to combat this scenario, provided the filters are well understood and do not eliminate what could be considered useful information for the neural network.

Since the quality of completeness ensures that the input and output interfaces of the neural network are completely described with regard to data format and performance criteria, the practitioner should make sure that preprocessing criteria are also established. Accuracy may also be something the practitioner examines to see if the data that the project expects to use have been defined with enough accuracy for proper preprocessing procedures to be set within the design stage.

3.4.2.4 Task: Criticality Analysis. Required Inputs: Task Report – Criticality, SRS, IRS.

In the Design Activity, the adoption of a neural network component does not cause the essence of the criticality task to change. Identifying the criticality levels is still primarily based upon a module's functionality and importance to the overall system criticality rather than being based upon the module's implementation.

Figure 17 represents a generic idea of how the practitioner may see the partitioning of the system containing a neural network.

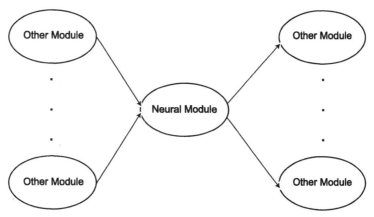

Figure 17. Requirements V&V: Treating the Neural Network as a Single Logical Module within the Overall System

Neural networks may take input from a single module or from several different modules. Likewise, outputs from the neural network might be used by a single or by several modules.

At this point, the criticality should be applied to the neural network module as a whole. Further refinement of the module may not take place until the design stage. For a more detailed breakdown, another generic example is presented in Section 3.4.3.4.

Criticality may also be assigned to rules or symbolic knowledge for neural networks. If the project elicits knowledge from domain experts, then the criticality of this knowledge can help in targeted training of the neural network [Kurd 2003]. This process can be part of the FHA outlined in Section 3.4.1.5.

3.4.2.5 Task: System V&V Test Plan Generation and Verification. Required Inputs: Concept Documentation (System Requirements), SRS, IRS, User Documentation, System Test Plan.

The IEEE Std 1012 identifies five areas the System V&V Test Plan should address. Of these five areas, addressing performance at boundaries and under stress conditions is where the practitioner should focus with regard to adaptive/neural network systems. Several of the tasks in the Design V&V Process address testing strategies and test data generation ideas for boundary and stress conditions, including Section 3.4.3.6 (Task: Integration Level V&V Test Plan Generation) and Section 3.4.3.7 (Task: V&V Test Design Generation and verification). The practitioner is encouraged to review the guidance for those tasks for techniques that will help to exercise performance at varying conditions.

3.4.2.6 Task: Acceptance V&V Test Plan Generation and Verification. Required Inputs: Concept Documentation (System Requirements), SRS, IRS, User Documentation, Acceptance Test Plan.

Acceptance testing validates that the software correctly implements the system and software requirements in an operational environment. For this task, the practitioner should determine the project plans for simulation development. Simulations will provide valuable experience in investigating the adaptive systems and how they might behave under expected operation.

There are many levels of simulations, but for acceptance-level testing this guidance recommends development of high-level fidelity simulations. High-level fidelity simulation configurations should provide the ability to use the adaptive system within the target hardware and communicate with all other external systems. Examples of high-level fidelity systems include advanced flight simulators (with simulated cockpit interfaces used by actual pilots), planetary exploration scenarios in locations that simulate the target environment, or multisystem computer networks emulating a component of the Internet.

By using the high-level fidelity simulation, the effects on the adaptive system from both normal and abnormal situations can be investigated. The simulation can help evaluate or facilitate the following types of testing situations:

- how long the system can adapt before encountering an error,
- effects on the system of communication time lags,
- performance in a target environment with different knowledge initializations,
- overall system handling of deliberate failures within the adaptive component, and
- human feedback from domain experts on the improvements, reduction or non-effect on performance due to the adaptive system.

3.4.2.7 Task: Configuration Management Assessment. Required Inputs: Software Configuration Management Process Documentation.

This task is concerned with determining the completeness and adequacy of the Configuration Management (CM) process for a project. In evaluating the CM process, the practitioner must evaluate many procedures, including whether software and document versions can be tracked, whether software and documents can be clearly identified, and whether changes to software or documents can be identified and managed.

For neural network systems, the configuration management procedures should be extended to include the special needs for each type of system as described below.

Configuration Management for Fixed Neural Networks. Within the configuration management plan, the practitioner needs to ensure that tracking of neural network training and testing data is complete. It cannot be stressed strongly enough that the step-by-step process of training and testing a neural network should be captured for later review or repetition. This is more important for fixed neural networks than for online adaptive neural networks. But whenever a project is performing some level of neural network training, the training process must be completely captured.

A project that does not accurately record which data was used during training, along with the order in which the training sets were applied to the network, will very likely lose the ability to retrain the neural network to the same specific knowledge representation. The project should also monitor the versions of the neural network after training. Tracking the neural network in this manner allows the developer to revert to a prior knowledge representation should later networks display incorrect results or undesired performance.

The following should be considered for tracking within a version control system:

- total training data set,
- total testing data set,
- each training set applied to the neural network,
- order of training set application, and
- neural network after training.

Configuration Management for Online Adaptive Neural Networks. The same consideration of training/ testing data can be taken for online adaptive neural networks, but this will be influenced by the planned design procedures for the neural network. If the project plans any pretraining of the online adaptive neural network before deployment, then certainly the training process needs to be captured and stored.

The practitioner may want to ensure that projects that experiment with different neural network designs capture that process within a version control system. Some projects, especially ones that are heavily research oriented, may have a general idea of the online adaptive neural network, but may not have all the specifics related to the network established at this point. There could be some resistance to this idea of completely documenting the experimental development process because of the time and effort required to trace the evolution of the system. However, a safety- and mission-critical project will have an easier time proceeding through safety review boards if it can explain the origins of the neural network and the steps that were taken to arrive at the current design.

Case Study Example 10. Neural Network Configuration Management

Some software releases of the IFC Program failed to include training data and describe training processes for the neural networks. As a result, these neural network builds could not be replicated.

Case Study Example 11. Version Description Document

Every release of adaptive software in IFCS GEN1 and GEN2 included a version description document (VDD). This document contained a detailed inventory of all neural network files, operational monitor files, and configuration files. It also included all neural network parameter values specific to that release.

3.4.2.8 *Task: Hazard Analysis.* Required Inputs: SRS, IRS, Hazard Analysis Report.

As hazard analysis within the Requirements V&V activity looks at the contributions to system hazards based upon software requirements, it should also assess system hazards introduced or modified because of the use of an adaptive system implemented by a neural network.

The software requirements documentation should contain requirements specifically addressing the neural network component(s) and these requirements can be used, as with non-neural network software requirements, to support the hazard analysis tasks during this stage. A project team experienced in neural network development will include better means of specifying neural network requirements and this will aid in determining their contribution to system hazards and in validating the control or mitigation of each hazard.

The initial hazard list generated from the PHI subinitial symbolic information and the FHA initial symbolic information in the concept hazard analysis phase should be considered when describing rules to be used within the requirements generation process. Unlike traditional software requirements that are intentionally complete, adaptive neural networks are incomplete due to typical real-world problems with insufficient data or knowledge prior to learning. This subinitial knowledge must be translated into logical rules. Thus a lack of knowledge, experience, and skill within the team of domain experts is a potential hazard that is critical to the requirements phase.

3.4.2.9   Task: Risk Analysis. Required Inputs: Concept Documentation, SRS, IRS, Supplier Development Plans and Schedules, Hazard Analysis Report, V&V task results.

When a project chooses to use neural networks, the identification of risks can be more difficult than with traditional software. Several factors should be considered: the project team's experience with developing neural networks, the complexities of the problem being solved, and the availability of adequate training/testing data. Risks that the practitioner should consider are:

Risks Associated with Development/Accumulation of Training/Testing Data. This risk can be considered a technical risk, but it may reflect the need for adequate managerial support. Proper development of both fixed and online adaptive neural networks requires that the project has in place a rich set of training and testing data. If the data sets are not yet collected, the project team will need to ensure that a sufficient set of data can be collected within the schedule. If the available data set is too small, proper knowledge accumulation may not occur, that is, the neural network will not be able to approximate the desired function well. The project may need to consider means of increasing the size of the data set, such as test data generation.

Case Study Example 12.
Requirements Risk
Analysis

The IFCS GEN2 system requirements risk analysis identified the rapid changes in design and software requirements as a potential risk. This included continual modifications to the design of the Sigma Pi neural networks.

Safety- and mission-critical systems may require a larger set of test data in cases when adaptive system designs are utilized. The practitioner will need to weigh the concerns of achieving a proper level of assessment on the performance of the neural network against what would constitute adequate testing data set size.

Risks Associated with Achieving Desired Neural Network Performance. This risk is a typical management concern. A potential impact to the project schedule is the time it may take to train the neural network to achieve specified performance levels. A project team can incorrectly predict the time it will take to achieve desired neural network performance if it does not have much experience with the intended neural network or the problem domain. Possible ways to mitigate this risk are the use of reliable neural network training tools, inclusion of knowledgeable neural network developers on the team, and the establishment of well-defined performance criteria.

3.4.3 Activity: Design V&V

IEEE Std 1012 describes the Design V&V Activity as dealing with the software architectural design (or preliminary design) and the software detailed design. When working with a neural network system, the practitioner is likely to encounter a different situation.

The preliminary design for the neural network may be a set of design criteria identifying the specific neural network architecture (multi-layer perceptron, competitive map, recurrent neural network, etc.) But this design may be simple and far from complete.

The neural network may progress through several training-testing stages in which the design becomes more refined. Unless a system is being reused or rehosted, training must take place to identify a good neural network design.

Because this guidance considers the design of a neural network to be different than the design of traditional software, it introduces a new task in Section 3.4.3.10 – evaluating the neural network design. The practitioner will also notice that an emphasis is placed on the development and correct use of the training and testing data sets for the neural network design.

3.4.3.1 Task: Traceability Analysis. Required Inputs: SRS, SDD, IRS, IDD.

During this task, design elements in the SDD and IDD are traced to requirements in the SRS and IRS, and requirements are traced back to design elements. The neural network design elements that pertain to control, such as the learning, growing, timing, and other aspects of performance, can be dealt with in a manner similar to other software systems. For the neural network requirements that pertain to knowledge, two additional considerations are suggested: construction of training data sets that reflect requirements and cover the input domain, and using rule initialization/insertion/extraction.

Special attention should be given to the development of training data sets. This is especially true for pretrained neural networks that are fixed before deployment. The training data set should reflect the software requirements that can be traced back to the system requirements and high-level goals for the system. Refer to Section 2.8 for a discussion on training set development.

After the training sets have been developed to reflect requirements and cover the input domain, it should be possible to train the neural network and extract a set of rules that can be used as a basis for the initial knowledge. It may also be possible to use the same training set to train other machine learners, such as a decision tree, against which to compare the extracted rules.

Tracing between design requirements and software requirements that pertain to the knowledge can also be assisted by the use of rule extraction techniques. Refer to Sections 2.3 and 2.4, respectively, for discussions of knowledge requirements and rule extraction.

The following steps can be taken to ensure traceability during the Design Activity. This process, started at the system level, carries through requirements into the design activity. The rules developed in this way ensure that the software requirements are traceable to the design of the neural network knowledge. (Note: the following steps are repeated in several sections of this guidance.)

- *Step 1:* Translate System Specifications dealing with the function, basic knowledge, and constraints of the neural network into initial symbolic information in the form of a rule base for the system. These rules can also include information from the Preliminary Hazard Analysis (PHA) and the FHA to address what the neural

network is not allowed to do or learn. These initial rules should be translated into
a format that can be inserted into the neural network (architecture specific).

- *Step 2:* Refine initial rules and translate them into software requirements. The
  process of refining the rules may include prototyping the neural network, inserting
  the initial symbolic knowledge, training the neural network to allow the rules to
  adapt to the training sets, and extracting the rules.

- *Step 3:* Translate refined rules into a format (neural network architecture specific)
  that can be inserted into the neural network.

3.4.3.2 Task: Software Design Evaluation. Required Inputs: SRS, IRS, SDD, IDD,
Design Standards.

Software Design Evaluation examines the SDD and IDD for several criteria including
correctness, completeness, and testability. All of these activities should be conducted
on the adaptive software design as well, evaluating the same criteria. These criteria do
not change nor do they become invalid because the practitioner may be applying them
to an adaptive system. For that reason, no new insight into conducting software design
evaluation is described for this task.

However, based on the type of adaptive system, there are additional criteria that will
need to be considered. For example, criteria based upon the selection of a neural network
system have been collected and placed into a new task that has been named Neural Network
Design Evaluation. Section 3.4.3.10 describes the Neural Network Design Evaluation tasks
and was written to follow the same style as the Software Design Evaluation task, but with
additional criteria specific to neural network designs.

The new task is specific to neural network design (as opposed to a general adaptive
software system design) because each adaptive technology is defined by its own
considerations. Practitioners dealing with techniques other than neural networks may
find useful guidance in the Neural Network Design Evaluation task, but will more likely
need to consult other texts dealing with the adaptive software technique used and create
specific evaluation criteria. The approach provided in Section 3.4.3.10 may prove useful in
directing the approach for a new task for the non-neural network, adaptive software used.

3.4.3.3 Task: Interface Analysis. Required Inputs: Concept Documentation (System
Requirements), SRS, IRS, SDD, IDD.

This task verifies and validates the software design interfaces for correctness,
consistency, completeness, accuracy, and testability. Along with the normal considerations
during the task there are two additional aspects to be considered when dealing with an
adaptive neural network system: pre- and postprocessing of the data used for learning and
operational monitor interface.

Pre- and Postprocessing Data.   An aspect of the neural network interface analysis
that should be given special attention is the pre- and postprocessing of the data. These pre-
and postprocessing functions may be considered as part of the neural network component
or system components that interface with the neural network. Preprocessing components
may handle the scaling of input information, the application of data interpolation or data
smoothing techniques, or identification of data to be used by the system based upon
data acceptance criteria. Postprocessing components may handle reverse scaling or data
smoothing.

Preprocessing of the data helps ensure that the neural network acquires the correct
knowledge during learning. Before the neural network is allowed to learn using the data,

the data is usually processed to adjust for the large variability in the different measurements used for the individual input variables. For example if both Mach and altitude were inputs to a neural network, there would be a problem with Mach having a range of [0-9] and altitude having a range of [0–50,000] (feet). Obviously, if these numbers were not scaled during preprocessing the number for Mach would be insignificant in comparison to the altitude number. This type of preprocessing is done to assure that no single variable overly influences the learning process.

Operational Monitor Interfaces. For the adaptive system, the interface with any operational monitor should be considered. Operational monitors, discussed in Section 2.6, are an important part of the overall V&V of the adaptive system. The interfaces between the adaptive component and its operational monitor should be examined with respect to all criteria mentioned in IEEE Std 1012.

Note that when the interface of the adaptive component changes, this will likely have a direct effect on the interface design of the operational monitor. For example, with the IFCS system, as the neural network underwent design changes and the number of internal weights changed, this directly affected the design of the confidence tool operational monitor.

Case Study Example 13. Neural Network Input Limiting

Both generations of IFCS limited inputs to the adaptive neural networks through preprocessing. In the adaptive system of IFCS GEN1, the lower and upper bounds for inputs, such as Mach and altitude, ensured the neural networks could only learn and operate within a limited flight envelope. The IFCS GEN2 adaptive system used a pre-processing protection scheme. This scheme tested groups of inputs to determine if any exceeded predetermined thresholds. If a violation occurred, a flag was passed to a specific neural network. This would disable learning for the specific time instance in that particular neural network.

3.4.3.4 Task: Criticality Analysis. Required Inputs: Task Report – Criticality, SDD, IDD.

Design V&V Criticality Analysis simply updates the criticality analysis conducted in the Requirements V&V Activity based upon the design documentation. The actual act of criticality analysis is no different for neural network systems than it is with a traditional software system. However, the breakdown of the neural network software may be something new to the practitioner. The following guidance provides general information on how a neural network may be partitioned for criticality analysis.

The manner in which the system design is partitioned for application of software criticality analysis can be different for a neural network system. The practitioner may see many possible subsystem partitions for a neural network system. At the highest level of abstraction, the neural network system may still be treated as a single module. At the lowest level, individual functional modules may be identified. Although this guidance cannot represent every possible scenario, Figure 18 depicts a likely scenario for identifying the software elements of an online learning neural network system.

The online learning neural network can consist of subsystem elements that handle the pre- and postprocessing of information into the neural network system. As mentioned above, the preprocessing functions could scale the online learning neural network inputs, compensate for missing information with data interpolation, or use data smoothing techniques. Postprocessing might perform some form of reverse scaling on the online neural network output to adjust the range of output values or apply data smoothing to

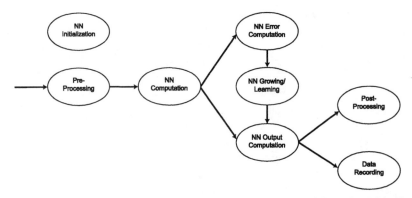

Figure 18. Possible Online Learning Neural Network Subsystem Breakdown for Criticality Analysis (NN = Neural Network)

the outputs. The online learning neural network may undergo some initialization whereby the network is given some level of previous knowledge, memory is allocated, processes are spawned, or some other form of neural network configuration occurs.

The online learning neural network will probably contain a growing/learning capability that will allow the network to gain knowledge over time. To facilitate proper growing/learning, the network may have an error determination module that is used to control when and, perhaps, on what, learning occurs.

One of the subsystem elements may be a module for recording data from the neural network. This module may save data to a solid-state drive or transmit

**Case Study Example 14.
Sample of OLNN Processes
from IFCS GEN1**

- *Configure DCS*
- *Clear DCS Networks*
- *Open DCS Config File*
- *Read DCS Parameters*
- *Scale Needed Parameters*
- *Clear DCS Initial Nodes*
- *Initialize DCS Networks*
- *Train DCS Networks*
- *Recall DCS Networks*

the data to somewhere else for record keeping. It is a strong possibility that such a module would exist for research applications and likely to exist for production systems merely to provide a means for later error analysis.

The fixed neural network is also presented here in a possible subsystem configuration to aid the practitioner. An example of a software element breakdown is shown in Figure 19.

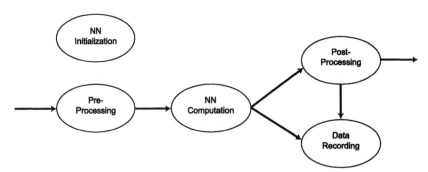

Figure 19. Possible Fixed Neural Network Subsystem Breakdown during Design V&V: Criticality Analysis (NN = Neural Network)

The fixed neural network contains fewer modules than the online learning neural network. Of importance are the modules dealing with the actual computation of the neural network, and the pre- and postprocessing functionality. The fixed neural network would probably contain an initialization capability along with a data recording capability for later analysis. The biggest difference between the two subsystem breakdowns is that the fixed neural network does not contain anything describing adaptation.

The above two examples do not consider systems making use of multiple neural networks. For those systems, the practitioner may see representations of individual neural network subsystems or submodules that comprise multiple instances of the neural networks. With whatever configuration the practitioner is confronted, the two diagrams above should serve as guidance for ways the neural network system can be partitioned.

Case Study Example 15. Sample of PTNN Processes from IFCS GEN1

- *Retrieve PTNN Input*
- *Parse PTNN Input*
- *Process Inputs*
- *Check Threshold Violations*
- *Process PTNN Networks*
- *Construct Outputs from Subnetworks*
- *Create Processed Output Array*

3.4.3.5 *Task: Component V&V Test Plan Generation and Verification.* Required Inputs: SRS, SDD, IRS, IDD, Component Test Plan.

The Component Test Plan identifies the schedule, activities, resources, and approach for testing at a component level. The guidance presented here is meant to aid the practitioner in the creation and evaluation of the test plan as it relates to the neural network design.

What items or features should be tested (linked to design elements)? At the component level, there are four aspects of the neural network design that the project can test:

- the neural network as a whole,
- the neural network structure,
- the neural network functionality (the source code that implements the network as a whole, including the transfer/activation functions, the input preprocessing, the output postprocessing, etc.), and
- the neural network knowledge.

Considering just the network structure, the testers may analyze the implementation of the various mathematical algorithms. As mentioned, these can include the transfer or activation functions, the summation functions, any input scaling or preprocessing, any output combination functions, and the growing functions. Testers may want to look for numerical instabilities that could come about from discretization of continuous functions or from improper or incomplete implementations. For example, hyperbolic tangent (tanh) is a commonly used function within a neural network. A project team may decide to implement a lookup table to approximate this function to save computational resources and reduce computational time. However, a lookup table is finite, and the tester may evaluate how the design deals with producing tanh values for a possibly infinite range.

Testers may analyze the knowledge acquisition process of online adaptive neural networks to determine qualities like speed of adaptation, limits to knowledge size, impact on existing knowledge from the introduction of new knowledge, and, once again, the underlying knowledge acquisition functions for numerical and logical appropriateness.

The other critical item to be tested is the knowledge within the neural network itself. Some neural networks may go into operation with no prior knowledge, and so this item may not be testable. But for fixed, pretrained neural networks or online adaptive neural networks that are given some *a priori* knowledge, knowledge testing will be important.

What will be the item pass/fail criteria? The criteria to evaluate a neural network system are not yet formalized for the purposes of verification and validation. There are often-used error metrics associated with neural network output, but these may not be sufficient for the practitioner. Some suggestions are presented within this guidance, but they should not be considered comprehensive. Examples are given for the four main areas of testing the neural network: neural network purpose, internal structure, functional construction, and acquired knowledge, if any.

Table 13 lists possible quality characteristic of neural network noted by Leung and Simpson [2000]. Neural network metrics are then required to provided quantitative measures of the degree to which the neural network exhibits the quality characteristics.

Table 13. Neural Network Quality Characteristics [Leung 2000]

Quality Characteristic	Description
Understandability (UN)	An indication of the magnitude of the various neural network's structural components, application data, and training elements
Modifiability (MO)	The ability of the neural network system to incorporate changes specific to individual experiments or applications
Testability (TE)	The verification and validation of performance of the neural network system for given applications
Applicability (AP)	The suitability of the neural network system to solve applications successfully
Consistency (CS)	The ability of the neural network system to reproduce consistent results from repeated experiments on the same application
Structuredness (ST)	The order and logic of the neural network arrangement
Scalability (SC)	The possibility of the training data being normalized or represented by data of a simpler type (e.g., real numbers represented by binary numbers)
Efficiency (EF)	The minimum effort or cost required to set up the neural network and training data set, and complete the associated training process
Complexity (CO)	The computational effort and storage involved in setting up and training the neural network system

Neural network metrics can be used as individual indicators of quality in the network structure and training. Table 14 presents a sampling of the various components of a neural network and the number of operations involved in training for a backpropagation neural network. These can be used as a set of metrics that measure the neural network's quality characteristics [Leung 2000]. The metrics can be used separately or mathematically combined to provide quantitative measures of the efficiency of the network and of the algorithmic complexity of a specified application problem.

Table 14. Neural Metrics in Backpropagation Neural Network [Leung 2000]

Definition of Metric	Quality Characteristic Measured
Number of input units	UN, ST, EF, CO
Number of hidden units on the kth layer	UN, ST, EF, CO
Number of output units	UN, ST, EF, CO
Number of layers	UN, ST, EF, CO
Number of iterations or epochs	TE, AP, EF, CO
Number of input patterns	MO, TE, CS, SC, EF, CO
Number of hidden weights on the kth layer	UN, ST, EF, CO
Number of output weights	UN, ST, EF, CO
Number of weights in the network	UN, ST, EF, CO
Number of scaling operations	SC, EF, CO
Number of activation function invocations	EF, CO
Number of addition and subtractions	EF, CO
Number of multiplications and divisions	EF, CO
Total number of operations	EF, CO

Criteria to evaluate the pass/fail performance of the neural network as a whole should take into account the neural network purpose. The obvious criterion here is the neural network error, which could be a single error function or comprised of several different error functions. A neural network testing case will contain an expected output for a given input. For neural networks that operate on continuous data, the error calculation will also be continuous. The function can be evaluated to determine if it falls below a specified threshold. It could also be evaluated based upon its shape or variance.

When evaluating the neural network structure, the practitioner may want to look at the memory requirements to hold the neural network. The practitioner will want to make sure that the memory utilization is examined for adaptive neural networks at expected maximum size. Likely, as the neural network grows, the corresponding computational time will grow as well.

For functional pass/fail criteria, the practitioner can look to numerical methods to determine evaluation metrics. Examples of characteristics that can be used to define the criteria are:

- computation time,
- accuracies,

Case Study Example 16. IFCS Neural Network Component Tests

Some of the early testing conducted in IFCS GEN1 and GEN2 ensured the neural networks did not:
- exceed specific memory requirements,
- retain knowledge after being reset,
- alter weights when in a non-learning state, or
- produce outputs in a disengaged state.

- precision,
- inspection for inappropriate non-linear characteristics within a continuous function, and
- inspection for improper interpolation between a discrete implementation of a continuous function (for example, a smoothness criterion).

The criteria to evaluate the acquired knowledge of a trained neural network can be similar to the criteria to evaluate the overall neural network. Proof of correct operation (and thus correct learning) can be evidenced through different operational error metrics. Additional knowledge criteria can be developed for the rules extracted though rule extraction techniques. These rules can then be assessed with their own pass/fail criteria such as number of rules, complexity of the rules (e.g., number of antecedents), or rule size (e.g., graphical dimensions – too large/too small).

What resources will be needed? Resources that the project will require for testing include neural network training and testing data. Resources that benefit the testing include visualization tools, neural network design tools, and simulations.

The very same tools involved in the development of the neural networks may be useful for testing purposes as well. MATLAB and Simulink, common development tools for neural network systems, allow testers to test the functions that comprise the neural network. If the neural network design is created as a Simulink or other graphical design, the testers may have to use the same system to perform testing.

Other testing needs can include source material that aided in the neural network design, like publications, neural network design books, or technical reports.

What personnel or training will be needed? The testing of the neural network components cannot be done without involving people who have a familiarity with neural networks. Although the test plan may or may not include the neural network developers, the practitioner should evaluate the test plan to make sure that test personnel responsible for designing and applying the test cases are familiar with the technology. Without some understanding of how to apply the test data sets, the selection of appropriate test cases and the evaluation of different neural network error and performance metrics, the test results could be misinterpreted or not insightful.

If neural network experience is lacking, use of neural network conferences, training seminars, or even online instructional materials may be helpful. There are many conferences dedicated to neural networks, intelligent systems, and artificial intelligence, and these conferences typically include one-day tutorials or workshops to introduce basic neural network background.

What should the schedule of test activities be? The target neural network will affect the testing approach and schedule for the project. For pretrained neural networks, testing will not be possible until the developers have finished the entire training, and the schedule will need to reflect that. For online adaptive neural networks with no knowledge or some knowledge before they are used, testing can begin as soon as the underlying architecture is final.

However, whereas complete module testing on a trained neural network may need to wait until the final design, testing of the individual functions that comprise the neural network can be attempted before the final knowledge is acquired. This, of course, assumes that the developers do not plan on changing or modifying the internal functionality of the network. This approach allows testing to begin earlier should the project schedule not be able to accommodate the expected duration of testing a completely trained neural network.

The traditional approach to testing a trained neural network is the application of testing sets to the network to determine the error between what the network has learned and the expected outcome of the test sets. The practitioner should expect that the developers will create these test sets, but the size of the sets may be impractical for practitioner purposes. If this is the case, the practitioner should incorporate into the schedule additional time to develop extra test cases.

3.4.3.6 Task: Integration V&V Test Plan Generation and Verification. Required Inputs: SRS, SDD, IRS, IDD, Integration Test Plan.

The integration test plan identifies the schedule, activities, resources, and approach for testing the integration of all software components into the total system. As part of the integration, the practitioner should ensure that the software modules that pass input into the network and those that use the outputs from the neural networks are tested while the neural network is in operation.

Integration testing for adaptive neural networks should identify if there are any abnormalities associated with receiving input or generating output in simulated system use. Of particular interest are the learning and growing algorithms.

What items or features should be tested? With regard to neural network integration testing, the important aspects that should be considered for testing include:

How the network handles all incoming inputs from every module that provides an input to the network (input analysis). An example of input analysis is the testing of the effects on the system from varying time skews that may occur in a real-time system (e.g., delays within communication busses, delays associated with another module performing some computation, etc.). Other test designs may investigate the effects of wide fluctuations in the magnitude of inputs, and neural network response to inputs at boundary conditions.

Integration testing also evaluates the correctness of any neural network preprocessing such as scaling and smoothing. For neural networks that require more than a few inputs, the practitioner is encouraged to ensure

---

**Case Study Example 17.
IFCS Integration Tests**

IFCS GEN1 and GEN2, integration testing was conducted under increasing levels of fidelity. A few examples of lower level fidelity testing include:

- testing that neural networks receive information correctly through the MIL-STD-1553B data bus;

- testing that neural networks process data at required frequencies; and

- testing that neural networks produce reasonable results.

For higher-level fidelities, the adaptive system was integrated with several F-15 components. A few examples of these tests include:

- testing the flight controller in response to varied outputs from the adaptive system;

- testing the adaptive system through simulated violations; and

- testing transients of the adaptive system through the pilot vehicle interface.

that the output order from all input-supplying modules aligns with the expected input order within the neural network module. A misleading situation can arise when a neural network has been designed with robustness and learns to accommodate misaligned inputs. The output may still qualify as meeting system requirements for correctness, but correcting the misalignment could lead to improved results.

How the network provides outputs to every module that requires an output from the network. As with the analysis of the effect on the neural network with time-varying inputs, the same effects should be allowed to propagate to the output for analysis of the effects of a time-delayed neural network output.

The same concerns about the input can be considered for the output. If the neural network is to postprocess the output, is the postprocessing correct? The order of the outputs to other modules should be checked as well, but experience indicates that output order misalignments are easier to identify than input misalignments.

Analysis of transients in the system. The practitioner should ensure that the test plan takes transients of the system into account. Analysis of transients in the system would be highly useful for systems that can switch from a neural network operation to a neural network nonoperation or vice versa. Such a scenario might occur in a research flight control experiment where the system can switch between a nominal flight control scheme that uses no neural networks and an enhanced flight control scheme in which the neural network is operating.

Tests can be designed to investigate if the neural network can handle possible input transients. Consider a neural network that has been designed to always learn. If the first few pieces of data it receives are zero before the system becomes activated, and then they suddenly change to useful nonzero values, how would the change from zero to nonzero affect the knowledge? The test could also look at the appropriateness of learning during transients: are zero values valid pieces of knowledge for the neural network to learn?

Analysis of the operational monitoring. If a project has made use of operational monitoring, integration testing needs to determine if the monitor is able to perform as expected. Possible aspects of testing the monitor include computational needs (highly important if the monitor resides on the same circuitry as a learning, growing neural network) and analysis to determine if the monitor can distinguish good performance from bad performance.

What will be the item pass/fail criteria? Within the integration test plan, the pass/fail criteria relevant to the neural network should have a higher emphasis on the neural network inputs/outputs and the effects on the neural network operation of being integrated with other systems.

Some possible criteria can be based upon:

- the production of outputs at a reasonable time (within system limits),
- the production of outputs that have correct shape/form/characteristics (no unreasonable non-linearities, no undesired variance, etc.), and
- the effect of transients from having the neural network turn on or off while the rest of the system remains in operation (for fault-tolerant or reversion systems).

What resources will be needed? The most significant resource needed for the integration testing is moderate-level fidelity simulations. Many projects would likely include such simulations anyway, but the practitioner may want to encourage augmentation of the simulations to allow for study of the items mentioned above, including the analysis of input/output time skews. Sophisticated, moderate-level fidelity simulations allow for analysis of the system under different stress conditions (with stress defined specific to the system), or different configurations of the neural network.

For systems that utilize operational monitoring, a moderate-level fidelity simulation would need to include the ability to simulate a failure in the neural network by turning it on or off, or deliberate corruption of the inputs/outputs. The testing of an operational monitor with the neural network can be difficult if there is a lack of *bad* data sets that encourage improper operation of the neural network. Some nontrivial time may be needed to create ways to make the neural network fail just to prove that the operational monitor scheme works.

What personnel or training will be needed? Personnel need to be familiar with the simulations that have been developed for the project. In some cases, this may be a complete software simulation, in others it may be a system that includes pilots, such as in a flight control system. Training may be required on how to maintain and use these simulations.

What should the schedule of testing activities be? Integration testing can only be done after the neural network has been fully designed. This means no additional training or knowledge content can be introduced into the neural network if it is to be pretrained.

3.4.3.7 *Task: V&V Test Design Generation and Verification.* Required Inputs: SDD, IDD, User Documentation, Test Plans, Test Designs.

The following suggestions identify methods that may be employed to generate test cases for the different aspects of testing. Details on the specific methods can be found within Implementation V&V: V&V Test Case Generation and Verification, Section 3.4.4.5.

Component Testing. At component-level testing, features that the practitioner should have tested include the unit level testing of the underlying neural network functions (transfer functions, activation functions, learning algorithms, and growth functions); the processing of the network inputs and outputs, an evaluation of how the network obtains knowledge (if it is online adaptive) and/or how its knowledge is correct given an operating environment; and performance analysis, including computational time and resource utilization.

Different visualization techniques are effective for interpreting the test results. Plotting the network error function against time is one of the most common and effective means of evaluating neural network performance. Plotting network node growth can give insight into how the network is growing and if the behavior is as expected or seems unusual. For example, with self-organizing maps, the test design may evaluate where the nodes are placed within a coordinate system. Since there are numerous neural network design packages and data display software, specifics are left up to the project and the practitioner.

Some of the techniques that can be used to refine the component testing approach include:

- *Automated test data generators* – Automated methods can be used to create significantly large sets of test data for reliability assessments, sensitivity analysis, or traditional brute-force testing. A common problem with neural network development is the lack of sufficient test data to support assurance for safety- and mission-critical systems.

- *Low-level fidelity simulations* – A low-level fidelity simulation of the neural network (or combination of neural networks if more than one work together) within a simulation environment can be used to contrast the testing results from an implemented neural network on an actual target system. Low-level fidelity simulations that allow for a layered inspection (such as module- and submodule-level views of the neural network design) can improve evaluation of the network operation.

- *Rule extraction* – For neural networks that have some amount of knowledge, extracted symbolic rules can aid the testers in designing test cases. An example is the use of symbolic rules to act as a form of data generation. If the rules are in mathematical equation form, randomly generating inputs for the antecedent part of the rule allows computation of a consequent. Consequents can be collected and formed into test data sets. As an example, consider the rule:

IF $(-4x + 2y \geq -16)$ AND
      $(-2x + 6y \geq 12)$ AND
      $(-6x + 0y \geq -48)$ AND
      $(7x + 2y \geq 46.5)$ AND
      $(2x + 4y \geq 28)$ AND
      $(-2x - 2y \geq -32)$

THEN $z = 0.2x - 0.1y + 1.7$

Now the values of x and y can be randomly generated. If, for an (x, y) pair, the values fit within this rule, z can be calculated and stored with x and y as an (x, y, z) data point that can be used for testing the system.

- *N-fold cross validation* – Cross validation is used here to refer to a testing technique that separates the available testing (or training) data into n parts, using $n - 1$ of these parts for training and reserving one part for testing. Consider one large available data set of 5000 pieces of data and the design of an online adaptive neural network. If five-fold cross validation is used, then the data set is divided into five parts, each with 1000 pieces of data. One part of the data, 1000 pieces, is set aside for testing and the other four parts, 4000 pieces, are used to train the neural network. This approach is then repeated four more times, excluding one part for testing and training with the other four parts. The results are then be compared for the five different runs.

Integration Testing. The purpose of integration testing is ensuring that the neural network is working well with the inputs from preceding modules and generating outputs correctly to the succeeding modules.

The evaluation of neural networks within real-time systems should focus on the effects of time lags to the network as well as the effect of missing data. For networks that are online adaptive, especially if they can grow, integration testing should evaluate the time to compute a network response or to adapt, as well as any possible time delays on network outputs.

If the system is using operational monitoring, the integration testing will determine how well the two designs work together. In some cases, the network design will dictate the operational monitor design, and if these two modules are developed by independent entities, interface problems can exist. One difficulty that the practitioner may see with integration testing of neural networks with monitors is that the networks never misbehave enough during testing to ever cause the operational monitor to flag improper behavior. Test designs may need to be developed such that neural network input is specifically chosen to cause misbehavior. In some, and possibly the majority of, cases, this will be difficult to do.

A technique that can be used within the integration testing approach is the use of moderate-level fidelity simulations. The moderate-level fidelity simulation can be the incorporation of the actual source code within the target computational environment. As with traditional software development, this can provide improved analysis of the neural network source code and how it will perform within constraints such as the processor, memory, and process scheduling.

As with the IFCS project, moderate-level fidelity simulations can include the use of additional test computers. The IFCS project used portable test computers that were specially equipped to interface to all of the research hardware and act as a user interface for system testers to evaluate and control the simulations and adaptive software. Instead of using the actual research hardware, a lab unit that consisted of less-ruggedized, commercially-oriented components was used. The lab unit provided all of the same functionality as the target hardware, but allowed system developers and testers to access the individual boards and interfaces to conduct analysis and evaluation. Lab units were also considerably cheaper and faster to create. Some systems may have the neural network software on a separate computer system to maintain a well-defined barrier between an adaptive/intelligent system and the other parts that may be more trusted. This scenario occurred during the IFCS project, in which the neural network code was separated from the flight control computers in case of errors. The flight control computer was considered more dependable and the project did not want any problems with the neural network to affect critical systems. Yet, the flight control computer fed inputs into the neural network and operated on the neural network outputs.

For moderate-level fidelity simulations, any input and output modules need to be simulated as well. A very basic means of accomplishing this is through the use of static input/output data files, as shown in Figure 20. The input is used by the neural network to produce its own outputs that are then compared against the static output file. The static file can be evaluated for correctness by practitioner-accepted means.

Several problems can arise when using static data files. First, there is an increased cost in time associated with developing static data files, especially the output data. Second, the use of static data limits some of the options the testers may have because any changes the testers may want to make will have to be delayed until new static data is generated. Third, there may be difficulty in producing the static data files, and a simulation may ultimately produce them anyway. Finally, the comparison of the static output data and the actual neural network output may have undesired discrepancies due to different hardware resources or different implementations.

A better approach than use of static data files is to simulate the input/output modules as shown in Figure 21. This approach has several advantages. Testers can modify test case generation more easily because they have access to ways of generating simulated input. This approach also makes it easier to insert data communication errors or data time lag problems to study the effects on the neural networks.

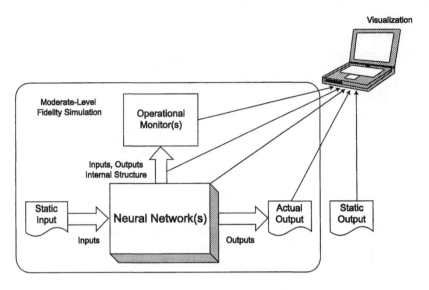

Figure 20. Moderate-Level Fidelity Simulation Using Static Data Files

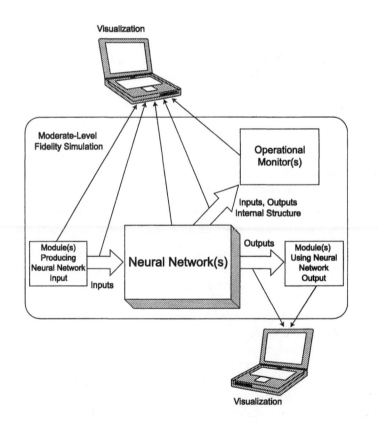

Figure 21. Moderate-Level Fidelity Simulation Using Simulated Input/Output

Of course, this approach has its drawbacks. The testers still need to generate input for the modules that feed into the neural network. Development of these additional modules for the simulation may be beyond project resources. And even if the simulations can be developed, there may be project concern, as there is with any simulation – the simulations may not accurately mimic their respective systems well enough to adequately test a high-assurance system. This is why the system test design discusses major-level fidelity simulations and the acceptance test design discusses high-level fidelity simulations.

Moderate-level fidelity simulations can aid testing of the operational monitoring schemes by allowing deliberate misbehavior of the neural network. If the simulations are designed in a manner that allows for direct manipulation of the simulation components, then deliberate errors can be introduced into the neural network knowledge content, structure, or functional behavior. An example of an environment that would allow easy simulation manipulation is a graphical programming language, like Simulink or one of the other neural network design packages.

Testing the operational monitors can also be aided by the use of rule extraction techniques. The symbolic rules can be compared to monitor rules to facilitate selection of input domain regimes that exercise the monitor. For online adaptive neural networks, knowledge rules can be purposely created to conflict with monitor rules and then used to provide a selection of training input for the network that will allow developers to ensure that the monitor will detect errors or anomalies.

System Testing. Specifically for neural networks, the system test design should ensure that the neural network design is compliant with the neural network system requirements, including the knowledge requirements.

System testing can be difficult due to a lack of well-specified knowledge requirements. If there are only few systems requirements related to knowledge, the system test design should focus on paying special attention to boundary data. As with the other test design, the use of symbolic rules (obtained from rule extraction) of a trained neural network or knowledge requirements can guide the generation of data near the system knowledge boundaries.

Another approach that can be used for system test design is the use of major-level fidelity simulations. An example of a major-level fidelity simulation is a software-in-the-loop simulation. These simulations have much of the software for the system operating in the exact system hardware, or in lab quality versions of the system hardware.

The testers who work with the major-level fidelity simulations may not be the same ones who worked on

**Case Study Example 18.
IFCS Run-Time Testing
Variations**

Tests were conducted for the GEN1 adaptive system under a variety of real-time conditions. This was achieved, in part, through the use of gains to alter flying quality dynamics, and limits used to disengage logic from the adaptive controller. The gain sets altered real-time control conditions to test the performance of the adaptive system under different sensitivities. At the same time, a corresponding set of limits ensured safe flying conditions by disengaging the adaptive system if limits were violated.

The GEN2 adaptive system used test sets. These sets consisted of different combinations of engaged and disengaged Sigma-Pi neural networks (roll, pitch, and yaw) with varied gains. During high-level fidelity simulations or flight tests, the pilot chose a test in order to engage individual or groups of neural networks with a predetermined set of gains.

the component-level testing and will probably not include the neural network developers. It is possible that the system testers will have very little familiarity with neural networks. Thus, communication between the testers and the designers is so important that it is recommended that the neural network developers participate in some capacity during system testing. At a minimum they need to evaluate the results from the neural network and judge their correctness.

Acceptance Testing. Acceptance testing is ensuring that everything works as specified within the final operational environment. A technique that can be used to refine the acceptance testing approach is the use of high-level fidelity simulations. The highest simulation would, of course, be the actual target system. As an example, the IFCS project ran tests on board the F-15 research aircraft as the highest-level fidelity by exercising parts of the system with the aircraft on the ground. Another example of the high-level fidelity simulation for this system was a Boeing hardware-in-the-loop facility that replicated the F-15 with an aircraft frame and allowed pilots to operate the aircraft in piloted software simulations.

3.4.3.8 Task: Hazard Analysis. Required Inputs: SDD, IDD, Hazard Analysis Report.

Hazards introduced during the design phase can vary greatly depending on the neural network architecture, size, intended use, available training-testing data, and other factors. Due to the nature of neural network development, the design and implementation phases are not as distinct as they are in traditional software development. Neural network development and training is usually a very iterative process of selecting training and test data sets, selecting the neural network architecture, training the network, and testing the network. For purposes of this book, the hazards specified for the design phase are those introduced from selection of training and test data sets and selection of the neural network architecture. Those hazards introduced during the actual training process for the neural network are described under Hazard Analysis for Implementation in Section 3.4.4.8.

Hazards introduced from the selection of training and test data sets include:

- Lack of adequate training and testing data is selected to achieve desired goals
  - For fixed neural networks, an insufficient set of training data leads to inadequacies in knowledge acquisition. The neural network is not able to generalize, or cannot provide an output that falls below an expected error threshold, or the largest error found under test is too high.
  - Large gaps exist in the input parameter space.
  - Training data set does not appropriately model intended goals
  - Undesirable patterns are repeated within the training data sets, leading to incorrect knowledge acquisition
  - Noise in the data set is presented in such a way that the neural network does not learn properly
  - Collection of training and test data sets is not documented
  - Lack of adequate testing data to achieve component-level project specific certification standards (i.e., while the neural network can be trained, the size of the available test data set is too small to achieve desired levels of confidence, or too small to comply with accepted testing standards)
- Neural network architecture is faulty
  - Neural network architecture is not completely specified

- Modeling assumptions are not appropriate for the problem
- One or more weights in the neural network is faulty
- The topology of the network is faulty
- The connections, in terms of existence and placement, are faulty
- Growing/learning algorithms are faulty, i.e., an inappropriate algorithm is selected for the problem
- Activation functions are faulty.

3.4.3.9 Task: Risk Analysis. Required Inputs: SDD, IDD, Supplier Development Plans and Schedules, Hazard Analysis Report, V&V task results.

Some of the management risks that may be encountered during the design life cycle include:

- impact to project because of insufficient training data,
- impact to project because of insufficient testing data,
- cost impact due to the need to purchase/obtain additional neural network development/analysis software, and
- loss of the ability to explain the neural network design.

It is possible that as a project progresses with the design and development of the neural network, that strict adherence to software engineering design and processes becomes lost and replaced with an *ad hoc* development routine that is neither repeatable nor explainable. It has often been said of neural network development that design is more of an art than a science. If the development team does not take all the necessary precautions such as controlling the training data, and recording design and training procedures, then it is possible that the end result, no matter how appropriate a solution, will be unexplainable and unlikely to be repeated should it become necessary. Repetition may be required should small problems be analyzed with the neural network linked to the application of specific training data sets or solvable by small tweaks to the original architecture. Without knowing how the knowledge went into the network, a design team cannot be certain that they will achieve a consistent and competent neural network product.

Technical risks at the design stage are related to the adequacy of the selected neural network algorithm, training and testing data sets, and the performance concerns in terms of computational time and space complexity. Selecting an appropriate neural network algorithm impacts the feasibility of system design and implementation. The process of selection is not well supported in the literature. Therefore, in most cases, system designers will need to define and apply selection criteria based on their level of experience with different types of neural networks, the availability of scientific literature and prior applications of the different types of networks in the given domain of interest. With respect to training and data set selection, these must represent the entire data domain, rather than just a few constrained examples. Especially in the case of safety- and mission-critical applications, the ability to demonstrate the performance of a neural network algorithm throughout the application domain is necessary for system acceptance. Lastly, different types of neural networks have varying requirements for computational resources. When a neural network is expected to contribute its results within the scope of a real-time application, computational complexity issues may significantly limit the choice of appropriate neural network architectures. For example, self-organizing maps (SOM) architectures typically assume that enough space will be available in the main memory to accommodate all the neurons required to represent the data domain. But the size of the available main memory is always limited, especially in on-board, real-time computers. If the neural network developers try to mitigate this problem by limiting the growth of neurons in an SOM, risk analysis should establish or verify convincing arguments that the limits will not adversely influence the SOM's ability to perform within the expected (required) function approximation error bounds.

3.4.3.10 Task: Neural Network Design Evaluation. Required Inputs: SRS, IRS, SDD, IDD, Design Standards.

This is a new task that has no mirror task within IEEE Std 1012. The Design V&V has a task associated with the evaluation of the design of traditional software that is better focused on evaluating concrete design elements not associated with adaptive software. Further, the existing IEEE Std 1012 task of software design evaluation does not account for the statistical learning characteristics of neural network software, failing to evaluate the setup and initial designs of the neural network before it is trained.

This new task attempts to address the adaptive nature of neural networks and their predesign before any training takes place. The practitioner will want to evaluate how the developers prepare the neural network for learning, what data the developers will use for training, and when to know that training is complete, among other items. The following criteria attempt to mimic the software design evaluation task by evaluating correctness, consistency, completeness, accuracy, readability, and testability.

Evaluating Correctness of Neural Network Design

Choice of Neural Network Architecture. The selection of the neural network architecture must be influenced by the problem that the network is being designed for, as explained in Chapter 4 of [Taylor 2005]. The practitioner will want to evaluate the selection process used to identify the basic neural network architecture (e.g., multilayer perceptron, self-organizing map, radial basis function, recurrent, Hopfield, etc.). Selection methods can be based upon empirical evidence, a down-selection based upon scientific comparison between multiple neural network types, or recommendations from within the field of neural network design (e.g., textbooks, papers, etc.). The practitioner should ensure that a project has sufficient evidence for the appropriateness of the neural network solution chosen. All reasons for the selection should be stated within the project documents, as early as the concept documentation.

**Case Study Example 19.
Choice of Neural Network
Architecture**

IFCS GEN1 and GEN2 requirements and design documents cited studies such as [Jorgensen 1997, Calise 2000]. These studies made use of similar OLNN architectures and structures in the same problem domain.

Choice of Initial Neural Network Structure. For fixed neural networks, there are at least three phases of the neural network design. The first phase is the initial design for the neural network. The designers will have chosen the architecture and have a general idea of the structure for the neural network. At this point, the practitioner may not have a solid grasp of the correctness or suitability of this initial design and will want to ensure that the design team has given proper thought and consideration to all choices made with regard to the neural network. This can be done through documenting team communications or the creation of a neural network design document. Practitioners should look for weak arguments for the initial design or lack of supporting ideas for the design. Even if the practitioner identifies these scenarios, the project can still proceed forward, but the practitioner may want to record these issues as risks that can have an impact on project schedule and success.

The second phase in the neural network design is an iterative process. The developers will be trying to tune the parameters of the neural network to achieve the desired performance. During this phase, the practitioner may want to ensure that the design changes are recorded along with reasons for the changes. Although it is quite plausible that the developers will try several different network topologies, the practitioner will want to be alert to developers who seem to make design choices that are not based on evidence or empirical results.

The third phase is the final neural network design. At this point, the neural network should have a detailed design regarding the neurons, layers, and connections. After the design is detailed, the practitioner should be watchful for design modifications. Modifying the neural network design after training can occur, but if the modifications become excessive or seem unending, the neural network design may never be complete. Excessive modifications can lower the accuracy of the neural network and can be an indication that the neural network developers are not sure of their design, which itself poses additional project risks.

Training Set. The practitioner may want to suggest the developers study the effect of any transformation that occurs on the inputs/outputs within a system on the performance of the neural network. For example, in some systems the neural network may operate on an embedded platform. This platform may accept inputs that are truncated or discretized. The input may come across a MIL-STD-1553B [1986] communication bus, a standard bus found in some avionics systems. This communication bus uses 32 bits for each message. If the original message is too large for the 1553 bus, then the message can be translated to fit within the 32 bits. On the receiving end, the message is then uncompressed for usage. In some situations, the compression-decompression can remove some granularity of the original message and even introduce errors of seemingly minor significance. The effects of this translation should be studied to prove that no ill effects occur during the performance of the neural network.

Training Process. The practitioner should verify that the training process, which should be clearly documented, has been written to correctly address the needs of the project. This includes identification of relevant training data sets, justification for the choice of the data sets, and consideration of the correct data formats for the training data.

Knowledge. Verify that the following steps were followed to assist in the development

Case Study Example 20.
IFCS PTNN Structure

Due to performance and accuracy concerns, the PTNN structure was divided into 34 separate multi-layered perceptrons to model the required 26 stability and control derivatives. For each of these 34 networks, the PTNN Design Report identified:

- input/output names,
- number of inputs/outputs,
- number of nodes in the first hidden layer,
- number of nodes in the second hidden layer (if any),
- total number of weights,
- total number of operations,
- number of activation functions, and
- origin of the design.

Case Study Example 21.
Selection of Learning Algorithm

Early studies in the IFCS Program compared different learning algorithms for the PTNN, such as Active Selection and Levenberg-Marquardt. Algorithm selection was based on resource requirements, network size, and error rates.

of the knowledge. (Note: the following steps are repeated in several sections of this guidance.)

- *Step 1:* Translate System Specifications dealing with the function, basic knowledge, and constraints of the neural network into initial symbolic information in the form of a rule base for the system. These rules can also include information from the PHA and the FHA to address what the neural network is not allowed to do or learn. These initial rules should be translated into a format that can be inserted into the neural network (architecture specific).
- *Step 2:* Refine initial rules and translate them into software requirements. The process of refining the rules may include prototyping the neural network, inserting the initial symbolic knowledge, training the neural network to allow the rules to adapt to the training sets, and extracting the rules.
- *Step 3:* Translate refined rules into a format (neural network architecture specific) that can be inserted into the neural network.

Evaluating Consistency of Neural Network Design. For consistency, it should be verified that the terminology use is consistent throughout the system documentation. Neural network terms such as *node* and *neuron* are sometimes used interchangeably and this could lead to confusion. A good practice is to provide a list of common terms and definitions in the system documentation. This provides a reference when reading and writing the documentation.

Evaluating Completeness of Neural Network Design

Performance Criteria. Verify that performance criteria are established in the SDD. For more information on possible criteria or neural network metrics, see Section 3.4.3.5.

Neural Network Elements. Verify that the specific elements of the neural network are defined and addressed in the SDD. Depending on the neural network type, examples can include nodes, connections, weights, activation functions, growth functions, learning function, hidden layers, inputs, and outputs.

Neural Network Knowledge. Verify that the knowledge the neural network may acquire during operation is outlined in the SDD. The methods for describing the knowledge are explained in the correctness section above.

Neural Network Training Set. The neural network designers use the training data sets as the basis for the neural network knowledge acquisition. Training sets obviously play a more important role in neural networks that are pretrained before deployment, but they can also have an influence on the development of adaptive neural networks that are not trained and fixed before deployment.

For pretrained neural networks, the practitioner should verify that the project has created a complete and sufficient set of data. Questions to be addressed in project documents include:

- Is the training data set of a sufficiently large size for assurance purposes?
- Have different sets of data been combined correctly to form the final training set?
- If data is missing, were interpolation or extrapolation techniques used to fill in gaps in the data?
- Is the data within the data set correct (e.g., proper format, appropriate)?

- Does the data cover the entire input domain of the problem?

Complete discussion of the proper creation of training data sets is beyond the scope of this guidance. Refer to Section 2.8 for additional considerations.

Training Process. The practitioner should verify that the training process has been defined within documentation. The process should include a description of configuration management (as used in the training process), the training data to be used, the procedures for applying the training data, identification of success criteria, and training process goals. In fact, it could be argued that in addition to design documentation, projects that perform any kind of training on the adaptive system should also develop Training Design documentation. By looking for clear and concise explanations of the training process, the practitioner is ensuring the project has identified a suitable training approach. It is very important that the project keep track of the training process through some type of versioning control system, as mentioned in Section 2.0 of this guidance.

Operational Monitor Design. Operational monitors will be used during testing and operation, but because resources are needed for developing and implementing them they need to be developed along with the neural network system. It is also necessary for design documentation to contain detailed information on the performance and interface of any operational monitors in order to minimize problems during integration with the neural network. Review Section 2.6 for an overview of operational monitors.

Evaluating Accuracy of Neural Network Design

Training set conforms to system accuracy requirements and physical laws. The training set needs to be evaluated for its accuracy given system requirements. Several questions can be used when evaluating this accuracy:

- Do the training sets conform to expected system usage?
- If the training sets come from a simulated system, does the data conform to expected system usage and physical laws? (that is, does this data make sense?)
- Is the precision of the data being used in the training set sufficient for project requirements?

Knowledge acquisition has adequate precision for system requirements. The accuracy of the neural network within the different development platforms (should they exist) should be compared and evaluated. Discrepancies between results of research implementations and actual implementations should be identified and analyzed. As might happen with any traditional software, once the neural network is installed on the target computer system, the results could have numerical differences from a development system. The practitioner should make sure that if there are differences (numerical inconsistencies past the fifth decimal place, for instance) that the project has analyzed the acceptability of such differences.

Evaluating Readability of Neural Network Design

Neural Network Design Report. There should be a separate design report generated for the neural network, the Neural Network Design Report. This document should contain a summary of all terms used for the specific neural network. Diagrams, flowcharts, and other appropriate visualization should be used to make the document easy to understand. Suggested topics for the content of the report are:

- Background Information – learning function, growing function, activation function, and stopping criteria
- Design Description – learning purpose, learning requirements, and learning interface
- Neural Network Implementation – configuration, source code, scaling, training, states, adding data, recall function, data recording, reset, saving, and restoration

> **Case Study Example 22.**
> **IFCS Neural Network**
> **Design Reports**
>
> IFCS GEN1 and GEN2 documentation included design reports for each of the neural network architectures. These reports included pre- and post-processing diagrams, learning algorithms, training processes, mathematical models, Simulink models, and results from very low-level fidelity simulations.

Evaluating Testability of Neural Network Design. Stability criteria should be established as objective acceptance criteria for the control functionality of the neural network. The stability criteria will be based on the mathematical equations that determine the timely convergence of the neural network learning.

Since the neural network knowledge itself can be considered as a design element, it is important that there are objective criteria established for validating it as well. If the system is adaptive, the criteria should also be incorporated in the operational monitoring scheme. The criteria to validate the knowledge could be rule based. The rule based criteria could be in the form of rule assertions that represent requirements or hazards to be checked against the internal knowledge of the neural network represented as a set of rules.

Other criteria related to the structure, weights, and connections of the neural network can be established.

3.4.4   Activity: Implementation V&V

During the Implementation Activity in the life cycle, design is transformed into code, data structures, and related machine-executable representations. A significant difference with neural networks (and learning systems in general) is that part of the realization of the design of these systems is in the knowledge that the system contains. The Implementation V&V Activity must be expanded to investigate not only how the neural network is coded, but what knowledge it has captured.

The Implementation V&V tasks address software coding and testing. The activities must verify and validate that these transformations are correct, accurate, and complete. There are nine tasks performed under the Implementation V&V Activity.

3.4.4.1 Task: Traceability Analysis. Required Inputs: SDD, IDD, Source Code.

During this task the V&V traces source code components to corresponding design specifications in the SDD and IDD, and traces the design specification back to source code. The neural network source code components that pertain to control, such as the learning, growing, timing, and other aspects of performance, can be dealt with in a manner similar to other software systems.

For the neural network knowledge, the traceability from source code to design specifications is more difficult. As the neural network learns and adapts, the changes that occur in the internal parameters and structure act like source code modifications. If the neural network is to be initialized with some *a priori* knowledge that represents the design specification, then this knowledge can be written in rule format and techniques used for rule insertion can be utilized to put the knowledge into the neural network source code. This supplies a trace for these specifications.

For networks that will be trained on data before deployment, the training sets can be developed around the design specifications. Traceability of the training data to the design specification may be accomplished by using machine learners on the training data. This can provide a way to develop understandable structures, like decision trees, that can be used to verify that the training data covers all areas of the problem domain. After the training of the neural network is complete, rules can then be extracted from the neural network and compared against design specifications and other structures that have been developed on the data.

The same type of changes that are made during initialization and training are also possible during operation for an online adaptive neural network. Therefore, there must be mechanisms in place to trace this changing knowledge that is acting like a source code modification back to design specifications. The use of operational monitors that are developed around the design specification can be used to assure that these specifications are continuing to be met during operation.

3.4.4.2 *Task: Source Code and Source Code Documentation Evaluation.* Required Inputs: Source Code, SDD, IDD, Coding Standards, User Documentation.

During source code evaluation, the practitioner may be presented with neural network source code that has been generated from autocoding capabilities of a software design environment. The IFCS system is an example in which neural networks were designed completely in a Simulink environment and then implemented into code through the MATLAB Real-Time Workshop autocoding capabilities. The code was unreadable and considered unmaintainable. Any changes had to be made in the Simulink environment, as changes to specific sections of the code were too daunting to be attempted.

Autocoding will likely complicate this task. Worse yet, some autocoding packages (like MATLAB's) provide little documentation and traceability capabilities, further serving to frustrate the practitioner.

Another aspect of this task that is unique to a neural network software system is the knowledge evaluation. Since neural network source code is only a part of what controls the neural network's behavior, it is equally important to examine the *training data* and the *training data documentation*. The training sets that are applied and the training process used should be clearly outlined in the documentation. Rule extraction could also be used to provide an understandable representation of the knowledge that the neural network contains at the time of deployment. Using these will give a better explanation of the operation of the neural network than just the source code alone.

3.4.4.3 *Task: Interface Analysis.* Required Inputs: Concept Documentation (System Requirements), SDD, IDD, Source Code, User Documentation.

All neural network inputs and outputs should be aligned with modules that send data into the network and operate on data that is generated by the network. It is very important that signal order and signal dimensions are verified because some neural network designs lead to robust systems capable of masking incorrect interfaces. These situations may give rise to minor errors that are easily ignored during testing because the error is not deemed noteworthy. Only inspection of source code for the modules communicating with the neural network will be sufficient to determine that the interfaces are aligned and of the correct units (i.e., degrees with degrees and not degrees with radians).

As mentioned in previous interface analysis sections, the functionality of preprocessing and postprocessing needs to be verified and validated against software and system requirements. As with the examination of input order and input type, all sources of neural network input should be checked to ensure that the assumptions about the preprocessing are correct. Likewise, modules receiving neural network outputs, including the operational monitoring, should be inspected to ensure that they have a consistent understanding of the data, as does the network when it postprocesses. If output data is being transformed, a module using the network output should know and correctly handle this transformation.

3.4.4.4 *Task: Criticality Analysis.* Required Inputs: Task Report – Criticality Source Code.

During neural network implementation, it is likely that the assigned criticality labels for the neural network are stable. However as the neural network, once realized, exists as software, there is a possibility that how the software was implemented and how the neural networks receive and transmit data signals can modify the criticality.

One way that criticality assignments can change is through the process of software reuse. As projects design and implement neural networks, it would not be unusual to reuse previously developed components of the neural network architecture. These components could be associated with the preprocessing, the implementation of a mathematical function, or the use of a neural network architecture library.

If these components have criticality assignments, those assignments might be considered to determine if they change in the current project. If the components do not have previously assigned software integrity levels, then the reused software might need to undergo software integrity assignment followed by an update to the neural network criticality analysis.

Interfacing technologies like the underlying physical medium or hardware also influence the assignment of criticality levels for the neural network during the Implementation V&V phase. The practitioner can consider the effects of how the neural network receives input data, how it communicates to subsequent modules within the system (perhaps modules operating on the neural network output in a control system), and how it communicates with operational monitors.

3.4.4.5 *Task: V&V Test Case Generation and Verification.* Required Inputs: SRS, IRS, SDD, IDD, User Documentation, Test Design, Test Case.

The practitioner should consult the previous tasks that discuss Component V&V Test Planning, Integration V&V Test Planning, and V&V Test Design. Many of the techniques discussed here have also been discussed within those sections. While those sections identified the techniques that might be used, this section will go into a little more depth describing how the techniques can be used.

Component-Level Test Case Generation. Historically, testing a neural network system has primarily relied upon the usage of the training-testing approach in which a set of available data is separated into a training set and a testing set. With this approach, the training set is usually three times the size of the testing set. After the neural network has undergone some level of training, the testing set is applied to determine overall network error.

There can be several problems with this approach. First, the use of a training-testing setup assumes that the project is either interested in development of a fixed neural network or in creating an online adaptive neural network that is going to be instantiated with some prior knowledge. It assumes that a neural network has been trained to some satisfactory degree such that the testing set can then be used to determine if the network's acquired knowledge is correct.

The second problem has only started to become more salient due to the slow migration of neural network systems into safety- and mission-critical systems. If the system is to undergo rigorous analysis and must demonstrate high levels of confidence of correct operation, this can imply that the testing sets will be quite large to facilitate testing such as reliability assessment. Traditional training-testing scenarios may not leave an adequate testing set size and the project can be at a loss as to how to achieve desirable levels of testing.

The project may want to consider some of the following techniques and options for component-level test case generation: automated test data generation, cross validation, bootstrapping, rule extraction, and low-level fidelity simulation.

The ATTG tool described in Section 2.7 has been shown useful in *generating test data* for a neural network. It has the ability to model nonlinear data based upon independent and dependent variables and then can use this model to generate new, statistically related data. This new data then can be used as additional test cases to test the neural network.

Because of the difficulty in matching nonlinear data, the models the ATTG creates are close, but not exact. This imprecision offers the ability to create new data that is different and perhaps entirely new to the existing neural network knowledge. For example, the tester could choose small perturbations of the independent variables, perturbations for which the models have higher accuracies, and thereby creating small deviations from the original data, thus allowing for a sensitivity analysis.

Another approach a tester may choose is to perturb the independent variables so the regressive models become imperfect, allowing for the creation of significantly different test sets with lower statistical relationship to the original data. This technique may introduce the neural network to entirely new sets of test data, even test data that may not totally exist within the operational profile of the system. Such data could allow the tester to examine how the system will react to anomalous data.

The tester may also want to use the trajectory-generating tool for the generation of data for brute-force testing of a neural network system. If the neural network system undergoing evaluation requires a certain level of confidence for an expected failure rate, then large sets of test data along with statistical analysis is the method by which to determine and verify that confidence. In some situations, the amount of test data needed to achieve that level of assessment will simply not be available to personnel. Use of the trajectory generator is one option available to try to increase the number of test sets.

Cross-validation and bootstrapping are both methods for estimating generalization error based on "resampling." The resulting estimates of generalization error are often used for choosing among various models, such as different network architectures.

In k-fold cross-validation, data is divided into k subsets of (approximately) equal size. The neural network is trained k times, each time leaving out one of the subsets from training. Then the omitted subset is used to compute the appropriate error criterion.

Note that cross-validation is quite different from the "split-sample" or "hold-out" method that is commonly used for early stopping in neural networks. In the split-sample method, only a single subset (the validation set) is used to estimate the generalization error, instead of k different subsets; that is, there is no "crossing." Although some people have suggested that cross-validation be applied to early stopping, the proper way of doing so is not obvious. The distinction between cross-validation and split-sample validation is extremely important because cross-validation is markedly superior for small data sets.

In *bootstrapping*, instead of repeatedly analyzing subsets of the data, you repeatedly analyze subsamples of the data. Each subsample is a random sample with replacement from the full sample. Anywhere from 50 to 2000 subsamples might be used. There are many more sophisticated bootstrap methods that can be used not only for estimating generalization error but also for estimating confidence bounds for network outputs. Bootstrapping seems to work better than cross-validation in many cases.

Rule extraction can be used to test the knowledge the neural network has acquired during training. Section 2.4 contains an overview of the rule extraction process. After training of the neural network has occurred, then rule extraction techniques can be used to extract a set of rules that represent the knowledge of the network.

Assertions, in the form of rules, can be formed based on identified hazards or system requirements. These assertions can be checked against the rules extracted from the network for consistency.

Low-level fidelity simulations offer the ability to simulate modules or even sub-modules within the system. A low-level fidelity simulation could be a stand-alone neural network simulation or the neural network with some basic input/output design to provide an analysis of the operation and performance of the neural network.

Low-level fidelity simulations may be designed in a language distinct from the target language of the neural network. Mathematical software design packages like MATLAB or Simulink allow the developer and the practitioner to study the system during adaptation or fixed operation. Chapter 7 of [Taylor 2005] identifies several neural network development packages that also allow the creation of neural network simulations.

Integration-Level Test Case Generation. Most neural network designs deal with stand-alone neural networks, or systems in which the neural network is run, and the system waits until the execution of the neural network is finished. Of course, this is not always true.

By experience, many safety- and mission-critical systems that use neural networks will be using the neural networks in a real-time system. Some other module in the system will generate or collect inputs for the neural network, and other modules will use or process the information produced by the neural network. The goal of generating integration test cases, therefore, should be to exercise the system in such a way to test that all modules communicate correctly with one another and that the neural network behaves properly. One method to accomplish this is through the use of moderate-level and major-level fidelity simulations.

An example of a major-level fidelity simulation is a SIL, in which all of the modules within the target system are present in some form of software. These modules could exist within computer workstations, lab versions of actual target hardware, or on circuit boards that are identical to the target system. Although the neural network software should be in the target language and properly compiled in the intended working environment, the other software modules do not necessarily have to be within the target language. Individual simulations might be used to represent some of the modules.

An integration test case would be some pre-chosen scenario that would execute the neural network and the system for specific conditions. For aircraft, these could be specific points within the flight envelope that were of special significance. For a vehicle health monitor, it could be at system stress conditions to determine if the monitor can detect an unusual event.

Test cases could utilize static data files as explained in the Test Design V&V section. The static data files can consist of inputs fed into either the neural network or into modules that provide neural network inputs along with expected outputs. These inputs and outputs could be collected by an entirely different system, perhaps even a lower-level fidelity simulation. The IFCS project used such a scenario in which test cases were generated in a moderate-level fidelity simulation that did not contain all system hardware and a simulated version of the neural networks. These data files were then compared to a HILS environment that contained hardware closer to the intended target.

When humans are involved in the simulation, as they were with the IFCS project, instead of striving for exact repeatability, another option is that of performing similar prescribed behaviors that can be repeated several times under different conditions. Within IFCS, since human pilots flew the F-15 experimental aircraft, instead of creating test cases that perfectly matched, the test cases consisted of a set of flying maneuvers, one after the other. Multiple pilots were used for different test executions, ensuring that test cases were unique. For these procedures, it was not as important to test perfectly consistent behavior as it was to test the system under similar circumstances, akin to sensitivity analysis.

Acceptance and System-Level Test Case Generation. As with the integration test case generation, the use of high-level fidelity simulations offers a good resource to generate tests to determine system acceptance and coverage of all system and software requirements. Much of the discussion in integration test case generation also holds for acceptance-level and system-level test case generation.

3.4.4.6 Task: V&V Test Procedure Generation and Verification. Required Inputs: SRS, IRS, SDD, IDD, User Documentation, Test Cases, Test Procedure.

One of the questions that arise in generating a test procedure is how to handle the stopping of a test and how to wrap up the test by restoring the environment. When testing an online adaptive neural network, the final steps in a test procedure could have an impact on future tests.

Presumably, with an online adaptive neural network, during the course of most tests, the network is going to adapt and gain knowledge. What the tester does with this knowledge can affect the results obtained from subsequent tests. Several scenarios exist for the way a tester can treat the neural network after it has adapted during a test:

- Abandon all learning acquired during the test and ensure that the neural network is reset to whatever level of knowledge it had before the test began. This scenario assumes that there exists a mechanism by which to reset knowledge or restore knowledge from a prior state.

- Maintain all learning and allow future tests to

**Case Study Example 23.
Restoration of Neural
Network Knowledge**

The IFCS adaptive systems have the capability to restore the OLNN to an earlier state. This was achieved by saving the state of the OLNN at preset intervals. This interval was adjusted as to not consume excessive computation time or internal bandwidth of the research computer. The detailed information saved from the OLNN allowed for offline analysis.

continue to modify the network knowledge through network adaptation. This test procedure would allow for investigation of the network over multiple scenarios to determine important neural network characteristics like duration of stability, duration of correctness, and rate of change of internal parameters.

- Maintain partial learning by some combination of network reset and continued network adaptation. It may be desirable to allow the network to acquire knowledge over a subset of the total test suite, but to have it reset periodically to determine the performance under different scenarios. Since the neural network knowledge is both a combination of its learning routines and the sequence of data with which it is presented, the network behavior may vary according to the order of the tests. For example, if there are four tests labeled T1, T2, T3, and T4, then what the network learns under T1, T2, T3, will likely be different from what it learns under T2, T3, T4 (with no presentation of T1).

3.4.4.7 Task: Component V&V Test Execution and Verification. Required Inputs: Source Code, Executable Code, SDD, IDD, Component Test Plan, Component Test Procedures, Component Test Results.

During this task, test results are analyzed to validate that the software correctly implements the design. Test results must also be traced to the test criteria established by the test traceability in the test planning documents. The component test results should be used to validate that the software satisfies the test acceptance criteria.

Section 3.4.3.5 identifies four aspects of the neural network at the component level that a project should test and provides possible criteria related to each of these. The four aspects of the neural network include: the whole, the structure, the functionality, and the knowledge. This section takes the four aspects and related criteria and suggests possible ways to analyze the test results.

One such criterion to evaluate the performance of a neural network as a whole is the error function. There can be one overall error function or several different error functions. These functions can be evaluated simply to determine whether they fall below a certain value or they could be evaluated based on rate of change or shape of the function. The Lyapunov stability analysis discussed in Section 2.9 is an example of an overall error function for neural network convergence. In Chapter 10 of [Taylor 2005], multiple functions are used to observe various aspects of a self-organizing map neural network to adequately assess its behavior during adaptation. These different error functions were used to evaluate best matching unit error, second best matching unit error, neighborhood error, and non-neighborhood error. These criteria provide an estimate of how well the weights and nodes in an adaptive self-organizing neural network are changing, given the application of the training data.

Note: The functions that are used to assess the neural network during implementation can also be used to develop the run-time monitors that will be used as validation tools during operation.

The structure of the neural network may be judged on criteria of size and complexity. For static-structure neural networks whose structures are fixed before deployment (such as a multi-layer perceptron), this will not be as serious a consideration. However, especially for neural networks that can grow during operation (such as self-organizing maps), size and complexity become important issues. There must be metrics in place to assure that the size and complexity of the structure will not overrun the memory or overextend the computational resources available. For neural networks that are allowed to adapt and grow during operation, there must be aspects of the design in place that will restrict the network from extending beyond computational resources. These aspects of the network should be fully tested on data sets of various sizes and complexities and results should be analyzed to determine how the network learns and grows in each situation.

**Case Study Example 24.
DCS Growth Limits**

For functional pass/fail criteria, numerical methods can be used to determine evaluation metrics. As suggested in Section 3.4.3.5, metrics can be designed around such criteria as computational time, accuracies, precision, non-linear characteristics, and interpolation between discrete values.

The criteria to evaluate neural network knowledge may include analysis of the neural network extracted rules and the training data set. In the case of neural networks, the design is implemented through the

In the adaptive system of IFCS GEN1, the DCS self organizing map neural networks were purposefully implemented without any dynamic memory allocation. This limited the amount of growth the neural networks could undergo to a predetermined static memory block.

actual software code and the knowledge that the neural network is allowed to acquire. If the neural network being implemented is trained and then fixed before deployment, it is advisable to analyze the training data set to determine if it fully covers all aspects of the problem domain. This may mean that the training set may need to be augmented to address different aspects of the problem domain. Training set analysis is discussed in Section 2.8. For these trained and fixed neural networks, the training data analysis is as important as the analysis of any other type of test results.

During the analysis of the neural network knowledge, it will also be useful to extract rules from the neural network. The rule information can be analyzed in several ways. The rules should first be compared against the neural network to determine agreement, making sure that they accurately represent the neural network. After it is determined that the rule extraction process has delivered a viable set of rules, this set can be a representative of the internal knowledge.

Domain experts can analyze the rules to identify discrepancies with intended design. Assertions that represent both requirements and possible hazards can also be developed in the form or rules and tested against the neural network. In the case of self-organizing maps, the rules may be used to identify boundaries for the neural network regions so that tests can be developed for boundary conditions. Visualizations of the rules can provide analysis of domain coverage. It is also possible to develop other structures such as decision trees on the same training set that could be compared against the rules.

3.4.4.8 Task: Hazard Analysis. Required Inputs: Source Code, SDD, IDD, Hazard Analysis Report.

Hazards introduced during the implementation phase are primarily related to the potential undesirable effects from the neural network learning the training data. Specific examples of hazards to be considered include:

- neural network adaptation leads to computational resource demands that exceed system resources, for example, the neural network requires too much processor time to compute, or requires too much memory to store all of the network structure;
- neural network takes too long to adapt to new stimuli, for example, the neural network cannot produce an output in the time required by the system;
- neural network training never achieves an optimal solution, for example, the

neural network oscillates between a value, converges too slowly, or has a higher degree of variance than the input data, etc.;

- improper utilization of training data, for example, the neural network is over-generalized and cannot provide a suitable solution to the specific problem;
- unable to qualify output fidelity across the input parameter space, for example, inappropriate output may be derived in areas where the neural network can not be trained in a supervised fashion; and
- observable behavior of the neural network is not predictable or repeatable.

3.4.4.9 *Task: Risk Analysis.* Required Inputs: Source Code, Supplier Development Plans and Schedules, Hazard Analysis Report, V&V task results.

The risks associated with the implementation phase of the neural network development process may fall into two broad categories: technical risks (such as improper output results) and managerial risks (schedule overruns due to underestimated processing time requirements and budget overruns due to unanticipated additional resource requirements).

Risks associated with the technical development of the neural network are generally considered the highest priority. The more traditional management risks, such as impact on cost and budget, tend to be less of a concern to neural network developers compared to more traditional software project developers because the magnitude of neural network development projects are generally smaller in scope. However, the cost and schedule for neural network projects may be adversely affected in cases when the project team does not have adequate expertise or neglects the importance of risks identified in the requirements and design stage analyses.

Both types of implementation stage risks, technical as well as managerial, are presented here as considerations for the practitioner. Some of the specific risks that can be encountered during implementation include:

- inability to assess inadequate neural network outputs and their impact to the overall operation of the system,
- impact on the project because of insufficient training data,
- impact on the project because of insufficient testing data,
- loss of the ability to explain the neural network design,
- schedule impact due to inaccurate estimate of the time required to train and test a fixed neural network,
- schedule impact due to inaccurate estimate of the time required to develop an acceptable online adaptive architecture,
- schedule impact due to inaccurate estimate of the neural network's computational time and space complexities, and
- cost impact due to the need to purchase/obtain additional neural network development/analysis software.

A critical success factor for a neural network is proper knowledge acquisition as a result of the training process. Use of operational monitors is suggested as a risk mitigation technique for detecting and potentially preventing improper knowledge acquisition. Several approaches for operational monitoring (e.g., data sniffing, Sensitivity Tool, Confidence Tool, comprehensive approach) of adaptive systems are presented in Section 2.6.

3.4.5   Activity: Test V&V

The Test V&V tasks address test execution and analysis of testing results. The activities must verify and validate that acceptance, system, and integration testing are defined, appropriate, and complete. There are seven tasks performed under the Test V&V Activity.

3.4.5.1 Task: Traceability Analysis. Required Inputs: V&V Test Plans, V&V Test Designs, V&V Test Procedures.

During this task, the traceability that must be verified is between the V&V Test Plans, Design, Cases, and Procedures. To verify correctness, a valid relationship between the V&V Test Plans, Designs, Cases, and Procedures must be established. To verify completeness there must traceability from all V&V Test Procedures to the V&V Test Plans.

The V&V Test Plans are completed for various levels at different times throughout the life cycle. The following is a brief summary list of considerations suggested in previous sections of the guidance related to the generation of V&V Test Plans and Test Designs. These items related to neural network testing should be carefully tracked to ensure that each of these items has associated Test Cases and Test Procedures.

Table 15. Summary of Test Plan and Design Suggestions

Level	Test Plan Suggestions	Test Design Suggestions (Section 3.4.3.7)
System	Fully test boundary and stress conditions for the neural network (Section 3.4.2.5)	Major-level fidelity simulations (SILS)
Acceptance	Test adaptive software on target hardware (Section 3.4.2.6)	High- and major-level fidelity simulations (SILS, HILS)
Component	Test four different aspects of the neural network design: the network as a whole, the structure, the functionality, and the knowledge (Section 3.4.3.5)	Visualization techniques for analysis of performance, automated test generators, low-level fidelity simulations, rule extraction, cross validation
Integration	Test four different aspects of the neural network integration with the system, including how the network handles inputs, how the network provides outputs, transients in the system, and operational monitoring. (Section 3.4.3.6)	Moderate-level fidelity simulations Development and integration of the operational monitor

3.4.5.2 Task: Acceptance V&V Test Procedure Generation and Verification. Required Inputs: SDD, IDD, Source Code, User Documentation, Acceptance Test Plan, Acceptance Test Procedures.

During this task, the Acceptance V&V Test Procedures are developed. There must be traceability established between the Test Procedures and the Test Plan. The Test

Procedures must also comply with the project defined test document purpose, format, and content, and satisfy the criteria of the Test Plan.

For an adaptive system, the Acceptance V&V Test Procedures should include procedures for accomplishing the acceptance testing using various levels of simulations. Acceptance testing validates that the software correctly implements the system. The use of major-level fidelity simulations (such as SILS), and high-level fidelity simulations (such as HILS) will allow the tester to observe the software in the operating environment and to validate that it correctly implements the system as it is allowed to adapt during operation.

For an adaptive system, especially one with integrity level 3 or 4, development of these major- and high-level fidelity simulations is of utmost importance. The development of simulations is an added burden for the project, however they are absolutely necessary in safety- and mission-critical cases and should be considered early and budgeted into the project.

Examples of major-level fidelity simulations include advanced flight simulators, planetary exploration environments, and computer network emulations. At this level, the procedures are designed to test the software components and integration in a test platform, usually the development platform rather than the final target hardware. The procedures developed for the adaptive neural network should assess criteria such as stability and convergence.

> **Case Study Example 25.**
> **IFCS HILS Flight Cards**
>
> The IFCS HILS test procedures consisted of a set of flight cards. Each card contained:
>
> - the initial conditions and configuration of the aircraft,
> - a series of flight maneuvers,
> - alterations in control gains, and
> - the state of the adaptive system.
>
> Similar flight cards used during HILS testing were used during the actual system flight tests involving the NASA F-15 aircraft. The pilots would perform the maneuvers on the cards while a control station on the ground monitored the entire system, ready to end the flight test if the system deviated from expected results.

A SILS can be used for major-level fidelity testing procedures. In these simulations, all of the modules of the target system are present in some form of software. These modules, at some point, should exist on lab versions of actual target hardware, or on circuit boards that are identical to those in the target system. Although the neural network software should be in the target language and properly compiled in the intended working environment, the other software does not necessarily have to be in the target language and some modules might be represented by simulations. The test cases at this level should focus on how the adaptive component performs as one part of the entire system. Issues of overall performance and timing can be assessed at this point.

The final level of simulation would be a HILS environment or testing on the actual target platform or hardware (e.g., a target aircraft on the ground, or with the new system running on the aircraft within a limited flight envelope). This high-level fidelity simulation will have all software modules in the system residing on identical, or near-identical, versions of the hardware.

3.4.5.3 Task: Integration V&V Test Execution and Verification. Required Inputs: Source Code, Executable Code, Integration Test Plan, Integration Test Procedures, Integration Test Results.

An online adaptive neural network should undergo several tests and the results should be analyzed together to evaluate proper operation. A few suggestions on documenting discrepancies between actual results and expected results are provided below:

- *Analyzing the results across increasing levels of fidelity* – The practitioner can analyze the neural network performance results observed while testing the interface as more and more modules are added to the integration testing. Look for performance degradations of the neural network as modules are added "in front" of the neural network. Performance degradation of even a few percentage points should be explained before continuing.
- *Results from deliberately switching the input order* – As a test, the inputs into the neural network might deliberately be switched and the performance analyzed to see if there are any substantial changes. One obvious consequence is that if any switch causes an improvement in performance, then it is likely that the inputs within the neural network are switched, or worse, the design may not be optimal.

3.4.5.4 Task: System V&V Test Execution and Verification. Required Inputs: Source Code, Executable Code, System Test Plan, System Test Procedures, System Test Results.

One way to analyze the results associated with system testing of the neural network is to evaluate the results that are generated by executing tests with the operational monitor in the closed loop. If the operational monitor should detect any problems, this might mean that the neural network is not operating within system requirements (even though the operational monitor is). As an example, consider a two-state monitor that either indicates a "go" or "no-go" situation. If the monitor during system testing ever exhibits a "no-go" indication, this result should be traced to determine if it is caused by neural network performance. If it is, then this could be an indication of failure of the neural network to meet system requirements.

The alternative to this analysis is that the neural network system is operating fine, but the operational monitor criteria it uses to identify allowed system states may be too narrow. Configurable operational monitors would allow for a wider range of system testing, and provide a means to eliminate possible nuisance indicators. Through the system testing, a better selection of monitor parameters may be achieved, provided that the project allows such modification during testing.

System testing over prolonged periods of operation may be able to point to problems associated with increasing needs for computational resources due to the neural networks. Results could be analyzed by looking for response time slowdown, excessive memory references, or other potential problems like significant hard drive usage. All of these could be symptoms of neural network learning and growing needing more resources than originally designated to those functions. If component-level and integration-level testing was conducted over short time periods, these results may not begin to manifest until system testing.

3.4.5.5 Task: Acceptance V&V Test Execution and Verification. Required Inputs: Source Code, Executable Code, User Documentation, Acceptance Test Plan, Acceptance Test Procedure, Acceptance Test Results.

Acceptance V&V testing can be carried out, as has been mentioned before, via major-level and high-level fidelity testing. Humans in the loop as part of testing the system may detect that the system as a whole is not performing as well as a previous system or as well as expected. Their experiences can be documented and perhaps used as feedback to the neural network developers to determine if the behavior is due to the neural networks.

Depending on the amount of configurability of the neural network during acceptance testing, the neural network may be able to change between predetermined setups. The testing may evaluate the setups to determine which one is more optimal. A part of analyzing the acceptance test results would then be to determine which configuration is the best.

With the IFCS, repeated simulations of the flight control system resulted in varying degrees of success, sometimes linked to the internal configurable parameters of the neural network. These parameters could be tweaked during the simulations, and sometimes the test sets involved different preselected configurations. Pilots were then able to remark on which system setup was the most favorable. This method of testing was used because it was difficult to establish optimal performance without pilot feedback.

3.4.5.6 Task: Hazard Analysis. Required Inputs: Source Code, Executable Code, Test Results, Hazard Analysis Report.

The hazards introduced within the V&V Test procedures, in general, are accepting or rejecting the adaptive system inappropriately. Many of these hazards are introduced by the development of the various level of simulations used in the testing procedures. The following are examples of the different types of hazards that may be introduced in the V&V phase:

- The Network Test Plan does not accurately reflect the Network Performance Specification and Data Analysis Documents.
- Not all phases of the development effort are critically reviewed for deficiencies:
  - failure to examine the original database for integrity,
  - failure to review preprocessing for accepted procedures,
  - failure to examine training databases for statistical bias in preprocessing activities,
  - failure to examine the training and testing phases for a rigorous and complete process, and
  - failure to examine the deployment phase to ensure that code generation was performed correctly.
- Developed test procedures for the adaptive neural network do not properly assess criteria such as stability and convergence.
- Not all of the modules of the target system are represented in some form of software.
- For SILS, the test cases do not accurately reflect how the adaptive component performs within the entire system.
- For HILS, near-identical versions of the hardware do not accurately reflect performance of the true hardware.

3.4.5.7 Task: Risk Analysis. Required Inputs: Supplier Development Plans and Schedules, Hazard Analysis Report, V&V task results.

For high-criticality applications, the reliable operation of the neural network is imperative. The most significant technical risk associated with the V&V phase of the neural network development process, especially for an adaptive system with integrity level 3 or 4, is a catastrophic failure of an accepted system. However, the impact to the project because of insufficient simulations that inappropriately reject the system would be significant cost and schedule overruns.

An example of a technical risk that could be encountered during V&V is loss of mission or life due to a system failure condition overlooked and, therefore, not analyzed in the test V&V phase. Management risks that can be encountered during V&V include:

- unavailability of adequate test and simulation equipment (hardware and software),
- unavailability of adequate operational test and analysis scenarios,
- cost impact from equipment damaged during testing, and
- cost and schedule impacts from reworking unnecessarily rejected system performance.

Testing during V&V must examine subsystems to assess performance during normal operation, operational degradation, functional failure, unintended function, and inadvertent function. Often, complete system risk assessment for adaptive systems is not feasible simply due to the many unknowns that may be created during the adaptive process. It may also be difficult to quantitatively determine the likelihood of a hazard within an adaptive system. However, the level of severity is usually easier to determine and may be adequate within the subsystem hazard and risk analysis to identify the effort necessary for risk mitigation. An example classification for risk assessment follows.

Class I: Catastrophic
    Unsurvivable accident with full equipment loss
Class II: Critical
    Survivable accident with less than full equipment loss; fatalities possible
Class III: Marginal
    Equipment loss with possible injuries but no fatalities
Class IV: Negligible
    Some loss of efficiency
    Procedures able to compensate; controller workload likely to be high until
        overall system demand reduced
    Reportable incident events such as operational errors, pilot deviations, surface
        vehicle deviations

A list of completeness criteria is also suggested for reference by the V&V team for evaluation of the neural network system as a checklist to ensure management and technical responsibilities for safety are accomplished. The completeness criteria address startup and shutdown, mode transitions, inputs and outputs, value and timing, load and capacity, environment capacity, failure states and transitions, human-computer interaction, robustness, data age, latency, feedback, reversibility, preemption, and path robustness.

3.4.6 Activity: Installation and Checkout V&V

Within the Installation and Checkout V&V activity, the acquirer of the software system receives the end product(s) and verifies that they have received the correct software and that the software installs and runs within a target environment. Testing done within this activity is to ensure that the software has experienced a correct installation and not to verify that it correctly implements every system or software requirement.

3.4.6.1 Task: Installation Configuration Audit. Required Inputs: Installation Package (e.g., Source Code, Executable Code, User Documentation, SDD, IDD, SRS, IRS, Concept Documentation, Installation Procedures, site-specific parameters, Installation Tests, and Configuration Management Data).

A component of the Installation Configuration Audit is the assessment of the completeness of the installation package to ensure that all software needed to correctly install and operate the system is present. Installation packages should include the adaptive system, including any online adaptive and fixed neural networks. The packages may also include run-time or operational monitors. In some scenarios, a different group than the one that developed the adaptive system may develop the operational monitors.

Installation packages may also contain the training data used and pieces of refined knowledge like symbolic rules that the system may use to reestablish a baseline of knowledge for the system as it adapts. If the system is designed to use knowledge refinement from a core set of rules and these are not included, the practitioner will have found a deficiency. Omission of training data does not itself indicate a problem, but it may mean that the project is limited in retraining of the system, and may mean that later projects lose the ability to redesign the same system. Further descriptions of the use of training data and refined knowledge are found in Chapter 2.

For a neural network system, the installation package may have two parts of the package that may not exist for other software packages: run-time environments (such as host software) and support files. These two parts may not be present in all neural network software, but they are discussed here to give the practitioner some examples.

If the neural network requires a run-time environment to operate within, the installation package will need to include any software that comprises that environment. This could be commercial software products such as MATLAB, Simulink, or another neural network development product. It might also include special libraries that include optimized mathematical functions or basic general neural network functions. The practitioner should ensure that the system is able to operate from the moment it is delivered until it is retired. Having valid license keys and checking that the licenses remain valid for the duration of the system operation can be easily overlooked.

Neural networks can be designed to work with support files and if so, they need to be included in the software package. Support files may take the form of header files that contain neural network weights or connection matrices. Specialized configuration files may also be considered as support files.

A configuration file may contain key parameters that the neural network will use during operation, such as how to initialize, how often to record data, ways to modify the internal functionality, or special commands to affect internal processing.

The evaluation of site-dependent or experiment-dependent parameters may be required for neural networks that require configuration files. Specific site-dependent parameters that may be included in the configuration files are definitions for gains that can be used on input signals or output signals and the selection of pre- and postprocessing functions for input and output data, should that be an option available to system users.

The IFCS F-15 system made use of configuration files with experiment-specific parameters. The values identified gains that were only valid for the particular flight-tests being conducted and controlled the limit of the neural network growth and the speed with which it was to generate recorded input.

Evaluation may take the form of simply verifying that the parameters found within the configuration file have been previously discussed by project engineers, software developers, managers, and end users. Confirmation may be required that these parameters have undergone system and acceptance testing with success.

An important part of evaluation of configuration files is to determine how the parameters can be modified and determining if there are policies in place to prevent erroneous modification of the configuration files. Such checks are necessary to prevent parameters from being changed without the consent of the end users and without the end users selecting values for configuration parameters that create hazards in the system.

3.4.6.2 *Task: Installation Checkout.* Required Inputs: User Documentation, Installation Package.

Once the neural network system is installed, operation on the target platform should be validated against the development system. Providing check cases as part of the installation package can help accomplish this task. The check cases allow the system installers to test that the system operates as it operated within the engineering/development environment and as it is intended to operate within the target environment.

If operational monitors for the neural network are part of the system, then there should be additional check cases for these components. During normal operation the monitor may not be fully tested, so check cases must be devised in a way to test that the operational monitor will catch abnormal or inappropriate neural network behavior.

If the neural network system is replacing a prior neural network system, it is recommended that tests be conducted to determine the affects the new software has upon the system. Special attention should be given to the inputs and outputs of the neural network, making sure any pre- or postprocessing is still being done correctly. Attention should also be given to checking that the system operates correctly and meets all system requirements. Specific changes or improvements in performance should be reported.

If the neural network (or adaptive) system is replacing a non-neural network (or nonadaptive) system, it is recommended that more rigorous testing be conducted. Additional testing can look at timing considerations like the system response times before and after the adaptive system is installed to verify that no ill effects will be introduced.

If the operational environment requires run-time licenses for the neural network software, the practitioner should make sure that the appropriate licensing agreements are included in the installation documentation. It should be confirmed that all entities involved in the operation of the neural network contain up-to-date licenses. The documentation should identify the period for which the license is in effect; this period should cover or extend beyond the lifetime of the system. This will remove the possibility that the neural network software stops working during system usage due to expiration of licenses.

3.4.6.3 *Task: Hazard Analysis.* Hazard analysis during Installation and Checkout must consider the contributions to system hazards introduced from incomplete or inappropriate installation packages, incompatible development and installation environments, and erroneous configuration files. As in previous phases, system hazards introduced from the use of adaptive systems or neural networks must be assessed. The following are examples of the different types of hazards that may be introduced in the installation and checkout phase:

- The adaptive system is not included in the installation package.
- Required run-time or operational monitors are not included in the installation package.

- Data is not included in the installation package.
- Inappropriate (erroneous, incomplete, or missing) training data is used in the installation procedure for reestablishing the baseline of knowledge as it adapts.
- Software required for run-time environments for the neural network is not provided within the installation package.
- Special libraries required for the neural network are not provided within the installation package.
- Neural network support files are not provided in the installation package.
- Incomplete or inappropriate configuration files are used within the installation procedure.
- Erroneous modifications are made to configuration files.
- Operation within the target environment is not compatible with the development environment.
- License keys for the system operation are not valid or have expired.

3.4.6.4   Task: Risk Analysis. Required Inputs: Installation Package, Supplier Development Plans and Schedules, V&V task results.

In general, the technical risks encountered during the installation and checkout phase is that the system either does not operate or operates improperly. Obviously, this type of technical risk is directly related to risks of adverse impacts on schedule and budget. Other risks must be of concern in this phase, especially when the neural network is part of a safety-critical system with the potential to terminate the mission or harm humans. In such a system, a minor incident can put humans at risk and escalate into budget cuts, schedule extensions, program delays, and even the cancellation of a program.

Risk mitigation during installation and checkout may be accomplished through a standard auditing procedure using documentation that provides a checklist of requirements for installation, including all system software, functions, special libraries, support files, and environment specifications. Check cases should be provided for operational monitors for the neural network. During replacement of a neural network system, inputs and outputs should be evaluated to confirm that pre- or postprocessing are done correctly. Acceptance testing should be completed to verify configuration file parameters. Additional system operations checks should be completed to ensure that system requirements are being met.

3.4.6.5   Task: V&V Final Report Generation. Required Inputs: V&V Activity Summary Report(s)

The Software Verification and Validation Report (SVVR) should document all of the activities that occurred during the previous stages of the life cycle, as is the case with traditional software. However, personnel creating this report should take special care to ensure that all discussions of the adaptive or neural network components are clear and easy to understand. In cases in which the discussion may require detailed scientific and mathematical information, the SVVR should give appropriate references to provide a basic background so readers who lack familiarity with the topic can achieve a better understanding.

3.5   PROCESS: OPERATION

The intent of the Operation Process is to evaluate use of the software within the target environment and requested changes. For adaptive systems, the purpose of Operation Process activities and tasks require additional considerations. Instead of a formal process in which changes are suggested, discussed, and possibly implemented, an adaptive system can change autonomously with little oversight. The Operation V&V Process needs to take this self-changing ability of the adaptive system into account by incorporating additional tasks and directions.

3.5.1   Activity: Operation V&V

The tasks found in the Operation V&V Activity are concerned with the use of the system within the target environment, the evaluation of desired changes, and routine operation of the system.

3.5.1.1   Task: Evaluation of New Constraints. Required Inputs: SVVP, New constraints.
      New constraints on the system may affect how a system is used or change the operating conditions of a system from those originally intended. The practitioner then needs to determine whether the system can still operate correctly given these new constraints.
      Areas in which new constraints can occur are listed below:

- *New knowledge requirements in the form of new areas of learning for which the system was not originally intended* – If an adaptive system is trained for a specific regime within the input domain, and then the use of this system changes to include another part of the input domain, this represents new constraints on the knowledge requirements. For example, an adaptive flight controller that was developed for use strictly after the plane achieved a certain altitude, later being expected to perform during takeoff and landing. The system may not behave as well within the new environment. Bad behavior can take the form of increased error on the output, removal of valuable basic knowledge, and improper learning/adaptation that causes the system to become unstable.
- *Input data arrives from a source different than originally intended* – An example of this scenario comes from the IFCS system. The neural network within the IFCS system uses the value of beta. Beta is recorded in three different places throughout the aircraft, with each value being unique. The research computer that hosts the neural network can be configured on the ground to accept beta over a digital communication medium or from an analog source. The designers intended the neural network to accept beta from a digital source, but ground support could change that, albeit through a very complicated procedure. A different beta with different characteristics could affect the accuracy and performance of the neural network system. The practitioner should consider the possibility of input changes (because in this case it didn't require a software change to cause the input change) and the possible effects on the adaptive system. One way to prevent possible problems may be the use of project wide policies that strictly enforce the changes ground control or other outside entities can do related to the inputs to the adaptive system.

- *Software that operates simultaneously as the adaptive system changes* – An example of this occurs when the adaptive system is one module of an entire CSCI, then new modules can be added or existing ones can be changed without causing the adaptive system to undergo maintenance. If this happens, system timing, throughput, and processing capabilities can change that affect the adaptive system behavior. The practitioner should inspect project plans to catch such scenarios.
- *Configuration files changes that control how the adaptive system operates* – This scenario is highly possible for research programs that want the ability to experiment with the adaptive system. The ability to change or modify how the adaptive system operates can be built into the system via the configuration files that are changeable, perhaps by ground support personnel. The practitioner should make sure the project understands these as new constraints and the possible impacts such changes will have.

Adaptive systems that can be configured can be changed without requiring another pass through the software life cycle. They can be changed directly by support personnel who install or operate the system during day-to-day operation. Because of this, any changes to the configuration should be treated seriously, and it is recommended that proposed configuration changes undergo a change review very much like the configuration control board process.

Changes to configuration should be examined to determine the effect they will have on not only the adaptive system, but also the system as a whole. Impacts can be to processor utilization, memory utilization, timing of data communication, and adaptive system stability. Any operational monitors may also be affected because new configurations could cause the adaptive system to operate outside of the expected limits imposed by a monitor, causing the monitor to no longer be relevant or to announce a large number of problems.

3.5.1.2 Task: Proposed Change Assessment. Required Inputs: Proposed Changes, Installation Package.

One change that may be proposed for an adaptive system is a change(s) to the system's knowledge. After operation, project personnel may identify areas of improvement that can be obtained by retraining the adaptive system or enhancing its basic knowledge. The practitioner should consider the impacts new knowledge can have on the adaptive system. Adding new knowledge could destroy or modify existing knowledge, and a better approach might be to reset the adaptive system knowledge and retrain it from scratch with the additional knowledge added into the training sets. New knowledge may also change the data storage requirements or the internal structure complexity of the adaptive system, making it unable to fit within the original computational resources.

Other changes that may occur include:

- changing the preprocessing or postprocessing functionality (e.g., input smoothing functions, removing or adding input vectors, etc.),
- changing the transfer function, activation function, growth functions, etc.,
- changing the internal structure of the adaptive system (e.g., adding a second hidden layer to a single hidden layer neural network), and
- replacing the adaptive system architecture (e.g., replacing a multilayer perceptron with a recurrent neural network).

Anything that changes the knowledge or structure of the adaptive system is likely to require all previous test procedures to be reapplied to the system.

Changes to the adaptive system may also have an impact on any operational monitoring that is used. New knowledge or structure constraints could cause the operational monitor design to become outdated and irrelevant.

3.5.1.3 Task: Operating Procedures Evaluation. Required Inputs: Operating Procedures, User Documentation, and Concept Documentation.

For this task, the practitioner must verify that the operating procedures are consistent with the user documentation and conform to the system requirements. The documentation and system requirements must address the adaptive capabilities of the system. In the user documentation, the users of the system should be made aware of aspects of the system that may be different because the system can adapt. If human operators are involved with the system, they should be informed and possibly receive additional training to deal with the adaptive system.

The practitioner should verify that the operating conditions are as expected by the adaptive system developers. The operating procedures, user documentation, and the requirements documents should detail the expected operating conditions for the system. If pretraining of the adaptive system has occurred then it should be verified that the pretraining aligns with the expected operating procedures and operating conditions.

The User Documentation should include information about the operational monitor and the updating of the monitor. This should contain a detailed plan of what to do when the operational monitor flags the adaptive system as unacceptable. There could also be plans to update the operational monitor based on analysis of performance data.

3.5.1.4 Task: Hazard Analysis. Required Inputs: Operating Procedures, Hazard Analysis Report.

Hazard analysis within the Operation process must consider the contributions to system hazards introduced from the operating procedures, the operating environment, and the adaptive system. It is important for practitioners to think about the unanticipated events that may occur as a result of the adaptive neural network system that are not typical in traditional software development efforts. The following are examples of the different types of hazards that may be introduced in the Operation process:

- user documentation is incomplete or unclear,
- operating procedures are inconsistent with the user documentation,
- operating procedures do not conform to system requirements,
- operating conditions differ from those intended by system developers,
- input data is received from a source that was not originally intended,
- pretraining of the adaptive system does not align with the intended operating procedures and operating conditions,
- basic knowledge is removed from the system by improper system behavior,
- memory limitation is exceeded,
- internal properties change such that response time exceeds an acceptable limit,
- new knowledge requirements in the areas of new learning for which the system was not originally intended,
- software operates simultaneously as the adaptive system changes,
- inappropriate changes are made to configuration files that control how the

adaptive system operates,

- outdated or irrelevant operational monitor design results from new knowledge or structure constraints,
- operational monitors function inappropriately as either too restrictive or not restrictive enough, and
- system becomes unstable from improper behavior.

3.5.1.5 Task: Risk Analysis. Required Inputs: Installation Package, Proposed Changes, Hazard Analysis Report, Supplier Development Plans and Schedules, Operation Problem Reports, V&V Task Results.

In general, the technical risks encountered during the Operation Process are similar to those in the Installation and Checkout phase, in that the system either does not operate or operates improperly. This is directly related to risks of adverse impacts on schedule and budget.

A suggested risk mitigation technique is imposing project-wide policies that strictly enforce a standard procedure for making changes related to inputs to the adaptive system. Risk mitigation during the Operation Process may include contingency planning for improperly behaving systems. Practitioners should be prepared to act when operational monitors indicate system performance problems. A top-level plan should be developed to detail the proper procedures for addressing system problems, including an investigation to determine whether the problems are within the system or within the operational monitors. Additionally, an action plan should be developed to detail steps to take to bring the system back to normal operation and when to take the system completely down. Likewise, a plan should be available to determine how to bring the system back online.

3.5.1.6 Task: Adaptive System and Operational Monitoring Performance Assessment.
Required Inputs: Installation Package, System with Acquired Knowledge, Operational Monitors.

This is a new task within Operation V&V called Adaptive System and Operational Monitoring Performance Assessment. The purpose of this task is to help reduce concerns a project may have related to the changing nature of an adaptive system. This task is more reasonable for a research system than a production system, but the guidance may be applicable to both. The evaluations that comprise this task can be included in the schedule and budget at the onset of a project.

Many of the recommended continual assessments can be used to define a set of requirements for operational monitoring. The operational monitor within the system can be designed to automatically monitor for project predefined conditions, thus completing the tasking described here. But in some cases, the level of effort done by the operational monitor may not be enough to satisfy project safety requirements, and additional tasking may be necessary to meet these requirements.

Some areas of operational monitor performance assessment include:

- *Evaluating operational monitor outputs* – The monitor can be assessed along with the adaptive component output to determine the number of true and false positives to determine operational monitor accuracy. If the operational monitor includes criteria that are too robust or too open, then the adaptive component may never be able to cause a condition that the monitor is looking for. Lack of any operational monitor "red flags" may indicate an irrelevant monitor. Periodic verification is

required to determine the effectiveness of the monitors.
- *Evaluating how often a threshold is approached by a signal* – One analysis evaluates if the adaptive component approaches a threshold or condition that the monitor is looking for, but never actually crosses a "red flag" boundary. This scenario could be interpreted in many different ways, but may be an important identification.

Assessing the performance at the level of individual adaptive component(s) within the system includes the following evaluations:

- *Evaluating component error* – Are the error values high for an exceptionally long time? Does the error have a high degree of variance? Does the error continually increase and decrease? Does the error slowly increase over time? All of these assessments may help identify the potential for hazards with continued operation.
- *Evaluating component resource utilization* – As the adaptive component learns, are the resources it uses beginning to overburden the system?
- *Evaluating component timing* – Is the adaptive system taking longer to produce an output or to learn? Are any time delays indicative of a potential problem?
- *Evaluating component growth* – If the adaptive system grows as it learns, does the growth increase at project expected levels? Is the growth a cause of strain on system resource utilization?

Assessing the performance of the adaptive system involves evaluating the entire system, including the adaptive component(s). Evaluating the system from a top-level perspective may reveal or eliminate causes for concern.

- *Evaluating system timing* – Does the system as a whole exhibit odd or unusual timing characteristics? Does timing of system events match design scenarios?
- *Evaluating system success metrics* – Does the system performance continue to align with expected system success?

3.5.1.7 Task: Periodic Test Execution and Verification. Required Inputs: Installation Package, System with Acquired Knowledge.

This is a new task within Operation V&V called Periodic Test Execution and Verification. The purpose of this task is to apply tests to the adaptive component and the system as a whole to evaluate new knowledge acquired by the system. This task is more reasonable for a research system that uses an online adaptive system than a production system, but the guidance may be applicable to both. This task is not essential for an offline adaptive system that does not continue to learn while in operation.

Periodic Test Execution and Verification only needs to be done for System, Acceptance, and Component testing. It should not be necessary to reevaluate the Integration testing because all system components should maintain consistent interfaces.

A part of this task may be the development of an updated System Test Plan or the creation of a new test document that outlines the tests that will be performed for Operation V&V System, Acceptance, and Component Testing. The test plan would identify when the system should undergo Operation V&V Testing and what parts of the system will be tested.

Because the adaptive component is allowed to learn, this periodic test execution and verification will test to determine if the newly acquired knowledge still meets system requirements.

3.5.1.8 Task: Proposed Knowledge Change Assessment. Required Inputs: Installation Package, System with Acquired Knowledge.

This is a new task within Operation V&V called Proposed Knowledge Change Assessment. The purpose of this task is to evaluate proposed changes to system-level knowledge after the system has been initially delivered and installed for operation.

This task closely mirrors the proposed change assessment task, which already exists within the Operation V&V activity. This guidance assumes that changes discussed during that task are more of a software (control) nature. The tasking described here is aimed toward the assessment required for changes made directly to the knowledge, which may or may not require a software change.

Changes that may be proposed include the following:

- *Inclusion of new knowledge* – Because system requirements can change, these changes may impact the input domain and thus the kind of basic knowledge that the adaptive system contains. Including new knowledge can impact the success of the system in remembering older knowledge. The project needs to determine what the specific new knowledge is, how to add this knowledge to existing knowledge, and the likely impact on prior knowledge. Testing will need to be revisited.
- *Removal of knowledge* – Sometimes, new knowledge may need to be removed. This could be because the project is conducting research and system researchers want to study if the adaptive system is consistent, or perhaps some piece of learned behavior is identified as being incorrect. If certain knowledge that has been acquired by the adaptive component is to be removed, this change creates many of the same concerns as does adding new knowledge. The project will need to define what knowledge is to be removed and how this can be carried out.
- *Reversion of knowledge to some prior state* – As with removing adaptive component knowledge, reversion of knowledge to some prior state may be a proposed change. Practitioners will want to make sure the project understands what the previous state of knowledge is; that is, do previous states exist and are they well defined? If previous states are recorded at intervals while the adaptive system operates, how is a reversion accomplished? The project should identify what the impact of a reversion is and if the system needs to repeat the testing activities.

3.5.1.9 Task: Configuration File Change Assessment. Required Inputs: Installation Package, Configuration Files, and Proposed Configuration File Changes.

This is a new task within Operation V&V called Configuration File Change Assessment. The purpose of this task is to evaluate proposed changes made to the adaptive system configuration files that alter the behavior of the system without requiring a software (control) or knowledge modification.

Configuration file change assessment is more likely to occur within a research environment than a production environment. System personnel who may not have been involved in the design and implementation of the system can make configuration file changes.

The use of configuration files to control system behavior may not be unique to adaptive systems. However, experience with adaptive systems development, especially in a research environment, indicates that configuration files are a likely way to control the system behavior, and protocols should be established to ensure that any changes made to configuration files do not have adverse effects.

This tasking recommends that the project establish a well-defined plan for who can change configuration files, when the configuration files can be changed, what parts of the configuration can be changed, and what oversight is required before a change can be made.

One way to accommodate this is to develop a system similar to a Change Control Board (CCB), to which configuration file changes are proposed and then evaluated by several members of the project. Evaluations should consider the intended benefits of a change and the possible ramifications. It is also suggested that simulation or system-level testing occurs on an experimental system to develop a model that describes the possible impact on the system.

All configuration file changes should be recorded and kept within a versioning control system so the system can revert back to a previous configuration. This would also allow problems to be evaluated, as the configuration setup that is related to the problem should be easily identified. Subsequently, each configuration file should undergo a release, including some piece of identifiable tag to designate configuration file versions.

3.6 PROCESS: MAINTENANCE

The Maintenance Process occurs when the software undergoes a change after the system has been delivered and installed, perhaps as a result of modifications suggested from the Operation Process. Only a single activity is defined for the Maintenance Process, the Maintenance V&V Activity.

3.6.1 Activity: Maintenance V&V

IEEE Std 1012 describes the maintenance of software as including the migration, modification, and retirement of software. The migration of software is the movement of a software system from one operational environment to another. This can be a concern for adaptive systems, especially if the transition of the system includes the movement of system knowledge from one operational environment into a new operational environment.

Modifying software involves some update to the software itself, perhaps as a result of uncovered problems with meeting requirements or the creation of new requirements. Generally, any modification should require that the software undergo the same verification and validation process. If the adaptive systems are modified, they should be checked using the same guidance provided in this book.

The retirement of a system occurs when a system is no longer maintained or used. The tasking associated with the retirement of a system does not seem to be affected if the system is adaptive or contains adaptive components. Because of this, only a few items will be suggested in the following sections regarding retirement of adaptive systems.

3.6.1.1 Task: SVVP Revision. Required Inputs: SVVP, Approved Changes, Installation Package, Supplier Development Plans and Schedules.

Revision of the SVVP and the subsequent SVVR are to be done based upon the proposed revisions/modifications intended for the software. The guidance found in this methodology should be consulted as needed, with updates conducted for all tasks based upon the presence of an adaptive system.

3.6.1.2 Task: Proposed Change Assessment. Required Inputs: Proposed Changes, Installation Package, Supplier Development Plans and Schedules.

The task of Proposed Change Assessment evaluates the impact that changes will have on the system, including the level of iteration required within the IEEE Std 1012 V&V activities and tasks. This guidance provides some examples to the practitioner of changes that may be proposed for the adaptive system and provides recommendations of the V&V activities and tasks that should be repeated. The list only includes changes that would require either a software modification (control) or a knowledge modification (knowledge). It is not all-inclusive, but the practitioner should be able to use the examples as a guide for other possible changes.

- *Assess changes to initial system knowledge* – A project may decide that the initial knowledge contained with the adaptive system needs to undergo change. This may mean that an initial system delivered with zero knowledge is now required to contain some rudimentary level of knowledge or that a system that contained basic knowledge now modify that knowledge somehow. Either way, this type of change would require the system to need retesting to ensure that the new knowledge still meets system requirements. The creation of the modified knowledge may require a redesign of the adaptive system and multiple iterations of training. The system could require re-implementation and operational monitor reassessment to accommodate the new knowledge as well.
- *Redesign of the adaptive system (for a neural network this would be number of internal neurons, number of hidden layers, a new connection matrix, new sets of initial weights, etc.)* – A complete redesign of the adaptive system may be a proposed change. Redesigns would require all V&V activities from Design onwards to be performed for the new system. This would include Design V&V, Implementation V&V, Testing V&V, and Installation & Checkout V&V. If there exists an operational monitor in use with the adaptive system, the operational monitor would need to undergo Testing V&V again to ensure that its performance with the modified adaptive system is still correct.
- *Operational monitor redesign* – If an operational monitor change is suggested, and the adaptive system itself does not undergo change, then the V&V activities of Design V&V, Implementation V&V, Testing V&V, and Installation & Checkout V&V would be repeated for the operational monitor system only.

3.6.1.3 Task: Anomaly Evaluation. Required Inputs: Anomaly Report(s).

An anomaly is defined as a behavior that is peculiar, irregular, abnormal, or difficult to classify. These behaviors are not severe enough to be considered as failures. One cause of anomalies for the adaptive system may be emergent behaviors as it continues to learn or adapt.

In a research environment, detection of an anomaly may come from a human periodically checking adaptive system performance and recorded data files and comparing behavior against that found within the design or testing environment. In a production or commercial system, detection may be captured as outputs from the operational monitor.

After the detection of an anomaly, the entity responsible for doing maintenance on the system should thoroughly investigate the situation by analysis of the data logs from the system or the operational monitor. The basis for the anomaly should be explained; it may be necessary to try recreating the condition in a test setting. Also, any safety implications and impacts should be ascertained. The anomalies should be discussed with development, management, and safety personnel and recorded so that comparisons can be made at future dates.

3.6.1.4 Task: Criticality Analysis. Required Inputs: Proposed Changes, Installation Package, Maintainer Integrity Levels.

Criticality Analysis conducted during the Maintenance V&V Activity assesses the software criticality levels of the proposed changes. This guidance assumes that the task of assessing the criticality of proposed changes is not affected by the existence of an adaptive component to a system. This assumption is in line with the previous sections in this guidance that dealt with criticality level assignment. Because of this, the analysis conducted during this task by a practitioner is very much the same, regardless of the existence of an adaptive component.

3.6.1.5 Task: Migration Assessment. Required Inputs: Installation Package, Approved Changes.

Migration assessment should undergo all the same steps for adaptive software as it does for conventional software. However, there is an additional consideration for adaptive system migration. The adaptive system will possibly gain knowledge during operation. It may be necessary or advantageous to capture and transfer this knowledge into the new system.

3.6.1.6 Task: Retirement Assessment. Required Inputs: Installation Package, Approved Changes, Project Documentation

The task of retirement assessment determines if the installation package defines the steps required to retire a system after it has been delivered. In terms of an adaptive system, this guidance identifies a few extra areas of consideration that go beyond the IEEE Std 1012 task.

Even though the software may be retired, the knowledge it acquires may be something that the project wishes to reuse within future systems or current systems through a migration plan. For adaptive systems, retirement assessment should determine if the installation package, approved changes, or project documentation addresses:

- how the knowledge acquired by the adaptive system undergoes retirement,
- if the knowledge can be extracted and passed on to other systems, and
- how the acquired system knowledge can be stored.

3.6.1.7 Task: Hazard Analysis. Required Inputs: Proposed Changes, Installation Package, Hazard Analysis Report.

Once modifications are made in the Maintenance phase to the software or to the knowledge, the practitioner should refer to the previous sections of this guidance to conduct the hazard analysis activities suggested.

3.6.1.8   Task: Risk Analysis. Required Inputs: Installation Package, Proposed Changes, Hazard Analysis Report, Supplier Development Plans and Schedules, Operation problem reports, V&V task results.

Depending upon the magnitude of change to the software or to the knowledge within the system during the maintenance phase, the practitioner should refer back to the appropriate phase to repeat the risk analysis process and risk mitigation techniques.

3.6.1.9   Task: Task Iteration. Required Inputs: Approved Changes, Installation Package.

The task iteration task should consider the inclusion of an adaptive system by using the guidance found in this book.

4

RECENT CHANGES TO IEEE STD 1012

The guidance provided in Chapter 3 follows the V&V processes, activities, and tasks defined in IEEE Std 1012-1998 [IEEE 1998]. An update to the standard was published in June 2005, designated IEEE Std 1012-2004 [IEEE 2005]. This updated standard contains a relatively small update over the 1998 version in terms of V&V tasks, the most significant change being the addition of a Security Analysis task. In the updated standard, revisions were made to clarify concepts and to reorganize a few of the tasks. No changes were made at the Process and Activity levels. This chapter presents a high-level review of the differences at the task level as they relate to the guidance provided in this book.

According to IEEE Std 1012-2004, the following changes were made to its Table 1 – V&V Tasks, Inputs, and Outputs:

- added "security analysis" to the required V&V tasks,
- reformatted test tasks to uniquely identify requirements for each test type – no normative changes were made to the test tasks,
- added a subtask to the "scoping of V&V" in the Acquisition support V&V activity to determine the extent of V&V on reused software, and
- corrected previous editorial errors.

Outside of the task changes, the change most significant to users of this guidance is the clarification of the concept of software integrity levels. Table 16 gives the four-level software integrity scheme used by the IEEE Std 1012-2004.

Table 17 shows the task differences between IEEE Std 1012-1998 and IEEE Std 1012-2004. Where a task name changed between the versions, it is denoted by adding "(changed)" after the 1998 task. Where a new task was added to the 2004 version that did not exist in the 1998 version, it is indicated by adding "(new)" to the 2004 task. Where an IEEE Std 1012-1998 task was removed in the updated version, it is denoted by adding "(deleted)" after the 1998 task.

Table 16. IEEE 1012-2004 Software Integrity Levels

Description	Level
Software element must execute correctly or grave consequences (loss of life, loss of system, economic or social loss) will occur. No mitigation is possible.	4
Software element must execute correctly or the intended use (mission) of the system/software will not be realized, causing serious consequences (permanent injury, major system degradation, economic or social impact). Partial to complete mitigation is possible.	3
Software element must execute correctly or an intended function will not be realized, causing minor consequences. Complete mitigation possible.	2
Software element must execute correctly or intended function will not be realized, causing negligible consequences. Mitigation not required.	1

Table 17. Task Differences, IEEE Std 1012 Versions 1998 and 2004

Process	Activity	IEEE Std 1012-1998 Task	IEEE Std 1012-2004 Task
Management	Management of V&V effort	1. Software Verification and Validation Plan (SVVP) generation 2. Baseline change assessment 3. Management review of the V&V 4. Management and technical review support 5. Interface with organizational and supporting processes	1. SVVP generation 2. Proposed/baseline change assessment (**changed**) 3. Management review of the V&V effort 4. Management and technical review support 5. Interface with organizational and supporting processes 6. Identify process improvement opportunities in the conduct of V&V (**new**)
Acquisition	Acquisition Support of V&V	1. Scoping the V&V effort 2. Planning the interface between the V&V effort and supplier 3. System requirement review	1. Scoping the V&V effort 2. Planning the interface between the V&V effort and supplier 3. System requirement review 4. Acceptance support (**new**)
Supply	Planning V&V	1. Planning the interface between the V&V effort and supplier 2. Contract verification	1. Planning the interface between the V&V effort and supplier 2. Contract verification
Development	Concept V&V	1. Concept documentation evaluation 2. Criticality analysis 3. Hardware/software/user requirements allocation analysis 4. Traceability analysis 5. Hazard analysis 6. Risk analysis	1. Concept documentation evaluation 2. Criticality analysis 3. Hardware/software/user requirements allocation analysis 4. Traceability analysis 5. Hazard analysis 6. Security analysis (**new**) 7. Risk analysis

Table 17. Task Differences, IEEE Std 1012 Versions 1998 and 2004 (Cont.)

Process	Activity	IEEE Std 1012-1998 Task	IEEE Std 1012-2004 Task
Development (cont.)	Requirements V&V	1. Traceability analysis 2. Software requirements evaluation 3. Interface analysis 4. Criticality analysis 5. System V&V test plan generation and verification (**changed**) 6. Acceptance V&V test plan generation and verification (**changed**) 7. Configuration management assessment 8. Hazard analysis 9. Risk analysis	1. Traceability analysis 2. Software requirements evaluation 3. Interface analysis 4. Criticality analysis 5. System V&V test plan generation 6. Acceptance V&V test plan generation 7. Configuration management assessment 8. Hazard analysis 9. Security analysis (**new**) 10. Risk analysis
Development (cont.)	Design	1. Traceability analysis 2. Software design evaluation 3. Interface analysis 4. Criticality analysis 5. Component V&V test plan generation and verification (**changed**) 6. Integration V&V test plan generation and verification (**changed**) 7. V&V test design generation and verification (**changed**) 8. Hazard analysis 9. Risk analysis	1. Traceability analysis 2. Software design evaluation 3. Interface analysis 4. Criticality analysis 5. Component V&V test plan generation (**new**) 6. Integration V&V test plan generation (**new**) 7. Component V&V test design generation (**new**) 8. Integration V&V test design generation (**new**) 9. System V&V test design generation (**new**) 10. Acceptance V&V test design generation (**new**) 11. Hazard analysis 12. Security analysis (**new**) 13. Risk analysis

Table 17. Task Differences, IEEE Std 1012 Versions 1998 and 2004 (Cont.)

Process	Activity	IEEE Std 1012-1998 Task	IEEE Std 1012-2004 Task
Development (cont.)	Implementation	1. Traceability analysis 2. Source code and source code documentation evaluation 3. Interface analysis 4. Criticality analysis 5. V&V test case generation and verification (**changed**) 6. V&V test procedure generation and verification (**changed**) 7. Component V&V test execution and verification (**changed**) 8. Hazard analysis 9. Risk analysis	1. Traceability analysis 2. Source code and source code documentation evaluation 3. Interface analysis 4. Criticality analysis 5. Component V&V test case generation (**new**) 6. Integration V&V test case generation (**new**) 7. System V&V test case generation (**new**) 8. Acceptance V&V test case generation (**new**) 9. Component V&V test procedure generation (**new**) 10. Integration V&V test procedure generation (**new**) 11. System V&V test procedure generation (**new**) 12. Component V&V test execution 13. Hazard analysis 14. Security analysis (**new**) 15. Risk analysis
Development (cont.)	Test	1. Traceability analysis 2. Acceptance V&V test procedure generation and verification (**changed**) 3. Integration V&V test execution and verification (**changed**) 4. System V&V test execution and verification (**changed**) 5. Acceptance V&V test execution and verification (**changed**) 6. Hazard analysis 7. Risk analysis	1. Traceability analysis 2. Acceptance V&V test procedure generation (**changed**) 3. Integration V&V test execution (**changed**) 4. System V&V test execution (**changed**) 5. Acceptance V&V test execution (**changed**) 6. Hazard analysis 7. Security analysis (**new**) 8. Risk analysis
Development (cont.)	Installation and Checkout V&V	1. Installation configuration audit 2. Installation checkout 3. Hazard analysis 4. Risk analysis 5. V&V final report generation	1. Installation configuration audit 2. Installation checkout 3. Hazard analysis 4. Security analysis (**new**) 5. Risk analysis 6. V&V final report generation

Table 17. Task Differences, IEEE Std 1012 Versions 1998 and 2004 (Cont.)

Process	Activity	IEEE Std 1012-1998 Task	IEEE Std 1012-2004 Task
Operation	Operation	1. Evaluation of new constraints 2. Proposed change assessment (**deleted**) 3. Operating procedures evaluation 4. Hazard analysis 5. Risk analysis	1. Evaluation of new constraints 2. Operating procedures evaluation 3. Hazard analysis 4. Security analysis (**new**) 5. Risk analysis
Maintenance	Maintenance	1. SVVP revision 2. Proposed change assessment (**deleted**) 3. Anomaly evaluation 4. Criticality analysis 5. Migration assessment 6. Retirement assessment 7. Hazard analysis 8. Risk analysis 9. Task iteration	1. SVVP revision 2. Anomaly evaluation 3. Criticality analysis 4. Migration assessment 5. Retirement assessment 6. Hazard analysis 7. Security analysis (**new**) 8. Risk analysis 9. Task iteration

Since the updates to IEEE 1012 are minor modifications, a practitioner wanting to use IEEE Std 1012-2004 and this guidance only needs to make correspondingly minor adjustments. The changes between IEEE Std 1012-1998 and IEEE Std 1012-2004 can be organized into four categories. The impact on the guidance for adaptive software systems is noted for each category:

1. *The addition of Security Analysis.* This is a new task added to the Development, Operation, and Maintenance Processes. Security Analysis evaluates the system at each stage from the Concept Activity (Development Process) to Maintenance with a security perspective. The guidance in this book does not address security. It is not clear how an adaptive software system would affect security, but it is likely that adaptive systems suffer from the same security risks that traditional software does. Adaptive systems make use of configuration files, files that hold parameters or weights, files that may contain logic or probabilities that allow for prediction or inference. The practitioner should consider their security implications.

2. *The addition of the Management V&V Task: Process Improvement.* Process improvement in light of adaptive software is not different from process improvement with traditional software. Additional or different processes may be used for adaptive software and these should undergo continuous improvement, as should any process.

3. *The removal of Proposed Change Assessment from both Operation V&V and Maintenance V&V.* The evaluation of proposed changes has been dropped from these two activities because the Management V&V activity now includes the evaluation of proposed change assessments along with the baseline change assessment. To address this change, the practitioner can refer to this guidance's proposed change assessment in Operation V&V (Section 3.5) and Maintenance V&V (Section 3.6) and combine it with the guidance for baseline change assessment within Management V&V.

4. *The separation of V&V test generation, design, verification, and execution into individual tasks for component, integration, system, and acceptance testing.* The IEEE Std 1012-2004, in explaining this change, states that no normative changes were made for each test type. The practitioner can follow the 2004 version by reading through this guidance and, when dealing with a specific type of test, looking for information that is either explicit (called out as a separate IEEE Std 1012-1998 V&V task) or is included as a subsection to an overall task. Table 18 provides a mapping that can be used for reference.

Table 18. Mapping Separated Test Tasks to Guidance Sections

IEEE Std 1012-2004 V&V Task	Guidance Section
Acquisition Support: Acceptance Support	Sections 3.4.2.6, 3.4.5.2, and 3.4.5.5, Acceptance V&V test tasks
Requirements: System V&V Test Plan Generation	Section 3.4.2.5, Requirements: System V&V Test Plan Generation and Verification
Requirements: Acceptance V&V Test Plan Generation	Section 3.4.2.6, Requirements: Acceptance V&V Test Plan Generation and Verification
Design: Component V&V Test Plan Generation	Section 3.4.3.5, Design: Component V&V Test Plan Generation and Verification
Design: Integration V&V Test Plan Generation	Section 3.4.3.6, Design: Integration V&V Test Plan Generation and Verification
Design: Component V&V Test Design Generation	Section 3.4.3.7, Design: V&V Test Design Generation and Verification, subsection on Component Testing
Design: Integration V&V Test Design Generation	Section 3.4.3.7, Design: V&V Test Design Generation and Verification, subsection on Integration Testing
Design: System V&V Test Design Generation	Section 3.4.3.7, Design: V&V Test Design Generation and Verification, subsection on System Testing
Design: Acceptance V&V Test Design Generation	Section 3.4.3.7, Design: V&V Test Design Generation and Verification, subsection on Acceptance Testing
Implementation: Component V&V Test Case Generation	Section 3.4.4.5, Implementation: V&V Test Case generation and Verification, subsection on Component Level Test Case Generation
Implementation: Integration V&V Test Case Generation	Section 3.4.4.5, Implementation: V&V Test Case generation and Verification, subsection on Integration Level Test Case Generation
Implementation: System V&V Test Case Generation	Section 3.4.4.5, Implementation: V&V Test Case generation and Verification, subsection on Acceptance and System Level Test Case Generation
Implementation: Acceptance V&V Test Case Generation	Section 3.4.4.5, Implementation: V&V Test Case generation and Verification, subsection on Acceptance and System Level Test Case Generation
Implementation: Component V&V Test Procedure Generation	Section 3.4.4.6, Implementation: V&V Test Procedure Generation and Verification
Implementation: Integration V&V Test Procedure Generation	Section 3.4.4.6, Implementation: V&V Test Procedure Generation and Verification
Implementation: System V&V Test Procedure Generation	Section 3.4.4.6, Implementation: V&V Test Procedure Generation and Verification
Implementation: Component V&V Test Execution	Section 3.4.4.7, Implementation: Component V&V Test Execution and Verification
Test: Acceptance V&V Test Procedure Generation	Section 3.4.5.2, Test: Acceptance V&V Test Procedure Generation and Verification
Test: Integration V&V Test Execution	Section 3.4.5.3, Test: Integration V&V Test Execution and Verification
Test: System V&V Test Execution	Section 3.4.5.4, Test: System V&V Test Execution and Verification
Tests: Acceptance V&V Test Execution	Section 3.4.5.5, Test: Acceptance V&V Test Execution and Verification

Appendix A

REFERENCES

Anderson, D., and G. McNeil. Artificial Neural Networks Technology, Data and Analysis Center for Software. 1992.

Andrews, R., J. Diederich, and A. B. Tickle. A Survey and Critique of Techniques for Extracting Rules from Trained Artificial Neural Networks. *Knowledge Based Systems* 8:373-389, 1995.

Boeing Phantom Works (BPW). F-15 Intelligent Flight Control System (IFCS) Hardware in the Loop Simulation (HILS) Procedure, IFCS-ARTS-HILS-003. 2003.

Bolt, G., J. Austin, and G. Morgan. Fault Tolerant Multi-Layer Perceptron Networks. Technical Report YCS 180, Advanced Computer Architecture Group, University of York, July 1992.

Calise, A., L. Seungjae, and M. Sharma. Development of a Reconfigurable Flight Control Law for the X-36 Tailless Fighter Aircraft. *Proceedings of the 2000 AIAA Guidance, Navigation, and Control Conference*, 2000.

Craven, M. W., and J. W. Shavlik. Visualizing Learning and Computation in Artificial Neural Networks. *International Journal on Artificial Intelligence Tools*, 1992: 399-425.

Craven, M., and J. W. Shavlik. Using Sampling and Queries to Extract Rules from Trained Neural Networks. *Proceedings of the 11th International Conference on Machine Learning*, 1994, pp. 37-45.

Darrah, M., B. J. Taylor, and S. Skias. Rule Extraction from Dynamic Cell Structure Neural Network Used in a Safety Critical Application. *Proceedings of the Florida Artificial Intelligence Research Society Conference*, 2004.

Gupta, P., and J. Schumann. A Tool for Verification and Validation of Neural Network Based Adaptive Controllers for High Assurance Systems. *Proceedings of High Assurance Systems Engineering (HASE)*, 2004, pp. 277-278.

Institute for Scientific Research, Inc. (ISR). Neural Network Evaluator Design Report for the Intelligent Flight Control Program. IFC-NNEDR-F001-UNCLASS-060904, 2004.

Institute for Scientific Research, Inc. (ISR). Toward Reliable Neural Network Software for the Development of Methodologies for the Independent Verification of Neural Networks. IVVNN-LITREV-F001-UNCLASS-11120, 2002.

Institute of Electrical and Electronics Engineers, Inc. (IEEE), Software Engineering Standards Committee. *IEEE Standard for Software Verification and Validation* (IEEE Std 1012-1998). New York, NY, 1998.

Institute of Electrical and Electronics Engineers, Inc. (IEEE), Software Engineering Standards Committee. *IEEE Standard for Software Verification and Validation* (IEEE Std 1012-2004). New York, NY, 2005.

Jorgensen, C. C. Direct Adaptive Aircraft Control Using Dynamic Cell Structure Neural Networks. NASA Technical Memorandum 112198, NASA Ames Research Center, 1997.

Kurd, Z., and T. P. Kelly. Safety Life Cycle for Developing Artificial Neural Networks. *22nd International Conference on Computer Safety, Reliability and Security* (SAFECOMP'03), 2003.

Kurd, Z., T. P. Kelly, and J. Austin. Safety Criteria and Safety Lifecycle for Artificial Neural Networks. Department of Computer Science, Internal Report, University of York, York, 2003.

Liu, Y., T. Menzies, and B. Cukic. Data Sniffing – Monitoring of Machine Learning for Online Adaptive Systems. *14th IEEE International Conference on Tools with Artificial Intelligence*, 2002.

Leung, W. K., and R. Simpson. Neural Metrics – Software Metrics in Artificial Neural Networks. *Fourth International Conference on Knowledge-Based Intelligent Engineering Systems and Allied Technologies*, 2000.

Miikkulainen, R., and M. Dyer. Encoding Input/Output Representations in Connectionist Cognitive Systems. 1988 Connectionist Models Summer School, Carnegie-Mellon University, Morgan Kaufmann, 1988.

MIL-STD-1553B. Aircraft Internal Time Division Command/Response Multiplex Data Bus. September 8, 1986.

NASA Dryden Flight Research Center. NASA Fact Sheet. http://www.dfrc.nasa.gov/Newsroom/FactSheets/FS-076-DFRC.html, 2004.

Perhinschi, M. G., G. Campa, M. R. Napolitano, M. Lando, L. Massotti, and M. L. Fravolini. A Simulation Tool for On-line Real Time Parameter Identification. *Proceedings of the 2002 AIAA Modeling and Simulation Technologies Conference*, 2002.

Reed, R. D., and R. J. Marks. *Neural Smithing*. Massachusetts Institute of Technology, Cambridge, MA, 1999.

Rodvold, D. M. A Software Development Process Model for Artificial Neural Networks in Critical Applications. *Proceeding of the 1999 International Joint Conference on Neural Networks (IJCNN/99)*, 1999.

Soares, F. Users Manual for the Generic Analysis Tool of Neural Network-Based Flight Control Systems, Hypersonic Vehicles, Adaptive Controllers, and Lyapunov Techniques. 2002.

Taylor, B. J. Regressive Model Approach to the Generation of Test Trajectories. Master's thesis, West Virginia University. Available at http://etd.wvu.edu/templates/showETD.cfm?recnum=1077. 1999.

Taylor, B. J., ed. Methods and Procedures for the Verification and Validation of Artificial Neural Networks, Springer, New York, NY, 2005.

Tickle, A. B., R. Andrews, M. Golea, and J. Diederich. The truth is in there: Directions and challenges in extracting rules from trained artificial neural networks, 1998.

Yerramalla, S., E. Fuller, M. Mladenovich, and B. Cukic. Lyapunov Analysis of Neural Network Stability in an Adaptive Flight Control System. *Proceedings of the 6th Annual Symposium on Self-Stabilizing Systems,* Lecture Notes in Computer Science, Springer-Verlag, 2003a.

Yerramalla, S., B. Cukic, and E. Fuller. Lyapunov Stability Analysis of the Quantization Error for DCS Neural Networks. *Proceedings of the 2003 International Joint Conference on Neural Networks,* IEEE Press, 2003b.

Appendix B

ACRONYMS

ACTIVE	Advanced Control Technology for Integrated Vehicles
ANN	Artificial Neural Network
AP	Applicability
ARC	Ames Research Center
ART	Adaptive Resonance Theory
ARTS II	Airborne Research Test System, 2nd Generation
ATTG	Automated Test Trajectory Generator
CCR	Change Control Board
CM	Configuration Management
CO	Complexity
CS	Consistency
CSC	Computer Software Component
CSCI	Computer Software Configuration Item
DCS	Dynamic Cell Structure
DFRC	Dryden Flight Research Center
EF	Efficiency
FHA	Functional Hazard Analysis
FMEA	Failure Modes and Effects Analysis
FTA	Fault Tree Analysis
GEN1	First Generation (intelligent flight control scheme)
GEN2	Next (2nd) Generation (intelligent flight control scheme)
HAZOP	Hazards and Operability Study
HLG	High-Level Goal
HQ	Handling Quality
I/O	Input/Output
IDD	Interface Design Document
IEEE	Institute of Electrical and Electronics Engineers, Inc.
IFC	Intelligent Flight Control
IFCS	Intelligent Flight Control System
IRS	Interface Requirements Specification
LEC	Lose Error Compensation
MLP	Multi-Layer Perceptron

MO	Modifiability
MUX	Multiplexer
NN	Neural Network
OLNN	Online Neural Network
PHA	Preliminary Hazard Analysis
PHI	Preliminary Hazard Identification
PID	Proportional-Integral Derivative
PTNN	Pre-Trained Neural Network
RFP	Request for Proposal
SC	Scalability
SDD	Software Design Description
SHL	Single-Hidden Layer
SILS	Software-in-the-Loop Simulation
SOM	Self-Organizing Map
SRS	Software Requirements Specification
ST	Structuredness
SVVP	Software Verification and Validation Plan
SVVR	Software Verification and Validation Report
TE	Testability
UN	Understandability
V&V	Verification & Validation
VDD	Version Description Document

Appendix C

DEFINITIONS

Term	Definition
Activation Function	A function applied to neural network internal calculations to produce the final output
Adaptive Component	A component of a computer software system that has the ability to change its configuration during operation
Adaptive Neural Network	A neural network that can adapt or change its internal structure during operation
Adaptive System	A system that changes its function, internal parameters, or realization while in operation
Backpropagation	The use of neural network errors during learning by passing the errors to the internal layers
Boundary Condition	A state that separates two distinct regions of the input domain
Configuration File	A file that is used to configure a system before use
Configuration Management	The control of changes, including recording thereof, that is made to the hardware, software, firmware, and documentation throughout the system lifecycle. In the context of adaptive systems, the focus of the configuration management process is on the recording of training data, and how the system was trained.
Convergence	The process by which a neural network reaches a stable state
Feedforward	Indicative of the forward propagation of inputs within a neural network, from the input layer through any number of interior, hidden layers, and then to the output layer
Fidelity	The degree of similarity between a simulation and the system properties being simulated

Term	Definition
Fixed Neural Network	A neural network that cannot change its internal structure during operation
Fixed System	A system that is deterministic and does not change during operation
Growth	A state of adding (or removing) neurons and neuron connections from the overall neural network structure
Developer	Any person responsible for the design, training, and implementation of the adaptive system/neural network
Hazard	A situation that is potentially dangerous to humans, society, or the environment
High-level Goals	Goals written for a system at the conceptual level
Failure	The inability of a system or component to perform its required functions within specified performance requirements
Fault	An incorrect step, process, or data definition in a computer program that causes the program to perform in an unintended or unanticipated manner
Functional Hazard Analysis	A formal and systematic process for the identification of hazards associated with an activity, used to identify potential safety-critical issues in hardware and/or software
Interpolation	Calculation of the value of a function between the values already known
Knowledge Acquisition	A method by which the neural network acquires knowledge through the application of stimuli
Learning	The modification of a neural network's behavior in response to its environment
Multilayer Perceptron	A feedforward neural network trained with the standard backpropagation algorithm
Neural Network	A mathematical model for information processing based on a connectionist approach to computation
Neuron	Basic computational element of a neural network
Operational Monitor	A secondary software application that runs concurrently with the adaptive software component to evaluate its performance during operation
Practitioner	The V&V or IV&V practitioner
Preliminary Hazard Identification	Process to identify any areas of concern. This should be carried out at the early stages of development, usually during project conception, and includes a systematic study of both operational and fault conditions.
Preliminary Hazard Analysis	This is a phase that takes the initial hazards identified in the PHI phase and subjects them to a detailed study using HAZOP or some other systematic technique.

Term	Definition
Risk	A measure of the probability and severity of undesired effects, often taken as the simple product of probability and consequence
Rule Extraction	A process used to develop English-like syntax that describes the internal knowledge of a neural network
Rule Initialization	A process of giving an adaptive neural network some pre-operational knowledge, possibly through early training or configuration
Rule Insertion	A process of moving symbolic rules into a network, forcing the network's knowledge to incorporate some rule modifications or additional rules
Self-Organizing Map	A type of neural network that can be visualized as a sheet-like neural-network array, the cells (or nodes) of which become specifically tuned to various input signal patterns or classes of patterns in an orderly fashion. The learning process is competitive and unsupervised, meaning that no teacher is needed to define the correct output (or actually the cell into which the input is mapped) for an input. In the basic version, only one map node (winner) at a time is activated corresponding to each input. The locations of the responses in the array tend to become ordered in the learning process as if some meaningful nonlinear coordinate system for the different input features were being created over the network.
Software Hazard Analysis	The identification of safety-critical software, the classification of potential hazards, and identification of program paths to identify hazardous combinations of internal and environmental program conditions
Stability Analysis	Stability analysis is the theory of validating the existence (or non-existence) of stable states. This theory is used to establish a mathematical foundation and proof of convergence for the neural network.
Support File	A file that is needed for proper operation of an adaptive system, often containing crucial information for the adaptive system to operate. Examples include configuration files and neural network weight files.
Symbolic Rule	A logical expression generally in the form of an if-then statement. In this context symbolic rules are used to describe the internal knowledge of the neural network.
Tester	Any person responsible for the testing of the adaptive system/neural network
Testing Data	Data used to verify that the neural network is performing as expected, often used after the neural network has been trained

Term	Definition
Threshold Function	An activation function that produces a 0 or 1 output signal based on whether the internal calculations of the neural network reach a certain threshold T
Training Data	Data used to provide the neural network with preoperation knowledge. This data allows the neural network to learn, by adjusting certain parameters, the appropriate response to predefined stimuli.
Transient	A condition that temporarily exists when the system moves from one state to another. During a transient, the system may enter into a suboptimal mode of operation, and conditions existing from the previous state could impact initial correct operation of the new state.
Weight	Numerical value attached to specific neuron input to indicate significance

Index

२